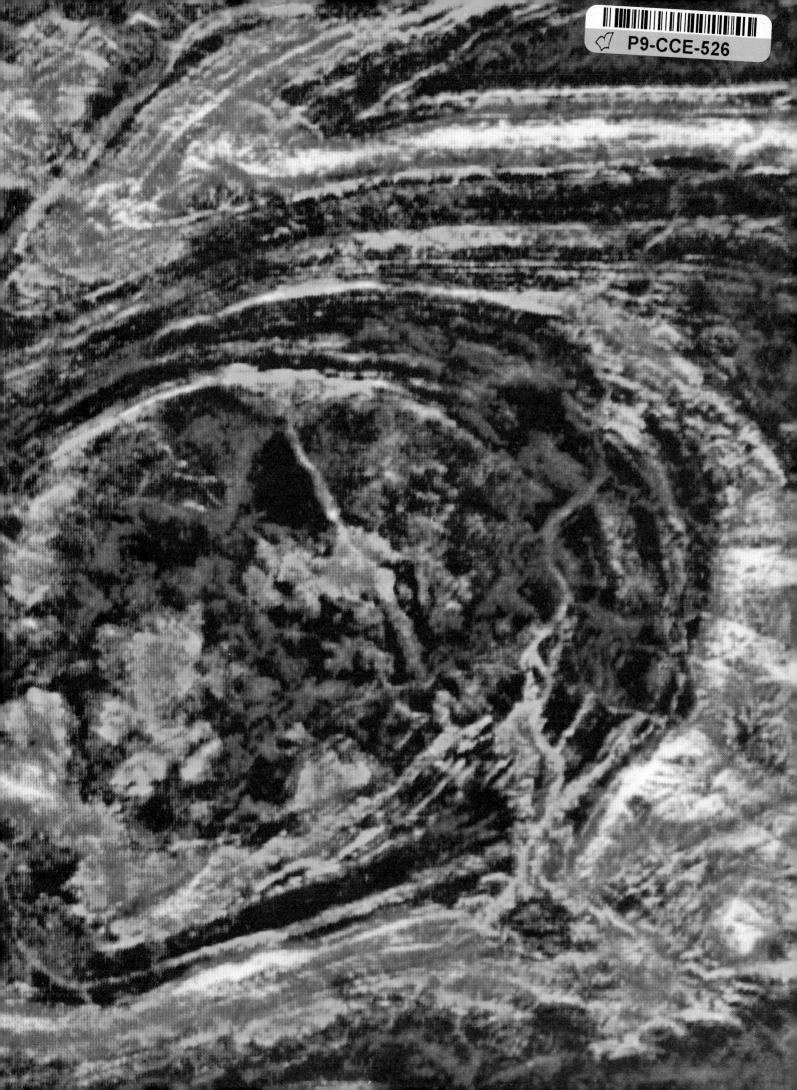

NASA
Views of Earth

NASA
Views of Earth

Robin Kerrod

GALLERY BOOKS
An Imprint of W. H. Smith Publishers Inc.
112 Madison Avenue
New York City 10016

Contents

Introduction

THIS BOOK WAS DEVISED AND PRODUCED BY
MULTIMEDIA PUBLICATIONS (UK) LTD
EDITOR: JEFF GROMAN
PRODUCTION: ARNON ORBACH
DESIGN: IVOR CLAYDON/BOB HOOK SUNSET DESIGN CO LTD
PICTURE RESEARCH: SPACE CHARTS

FIRST PUBLISHED IN THE UNITED STATES OF AMERICA 1985 BY
GALLERY BOOKS, AN IMPRINT OF W. H. SMITH PUBLISHERS INC.,
112 MADISON AVENUE, NEW YORK, NY 10016
ISBN 0 8317 6310 8
TYPESET BY ROWLAND PHOTOTYPESETTING (LONDON) LTD
ORIGINATION BY IMAGO
PRINTED IN ITALY BY SAGDOS

Half-title page: Sediment-laden waters around China's Luichow peninsula (top), (Landsat MSS).

Title page: A false-color image of the Cornish coast of England, created by Landsat's thematic mapper.

These pages: A more distant view of Earth, snapped by the Apollo 8 astronauts in December 1968.

Introduction

On May 15, 1963 astronaut Gordon Cooper blasted off the launch pad at Cape Canaveral in the Mercury 9 space capsule. He was going to break the American record by spending a total of 34 hours in orbit; circling the Earth 22 times. Unlike the previous Mercury astronauts, he had time to take a closer look at the Earth's landscape, slowly unfolding some 150 miles (240 km) beneath him. What he reported left mission control and Earth scientists incredulous.

Cooper said he could see individual houses and streets in low-humidity and cloudless areas, such as the Tibetan plain and the south-western United States. A steam locomotive puffing along a railroad track in India. A vehicle kicking up the dust along a highway in Arizona. The wake of a boat on a Burmese river.

Frankly, everyone back on Earth was sceptical. They suspected that Cooper might be having mild hallucinations, and no doubt wondered whether this was to be a problem on longer space flights. When the Gemini missions began in 1965, however, the truth of Cooper's observations was revealed. Incredible details can be seen from orbit. The implications of this excited the scientific community, and were not, of course, lost on the military. So on subsequent Gemini and some Apollo missions, Earth photography became a regular activity.

Electronic Eyes

Astronauts still do take remarkable pictures from orbit on ordinary color film, but the greatest wealth of knowledge about the Earth's surface has come from instruments on board unmanned satellites, which view the Earth in light of many different wavelengths. The most notable of these is NASA's Landsat series. Landsat does not take actual photographs of the Earth, but forms electronic images as it scans the ground in narrow strips. The image data are transmitted back to ground stations, where they are converted, through ingenious computer wizardry, into fascinating false-color pictures.

These pictures reveal a wealth of detail about the nature and use of the land. They reveal large-scale rock formations that can help pinpoint new mineral deposits. They can show where disease is rife in growing crops. They can spot where fields have been plowed; where harvesting is taking place; where forest fires have devastated the landscape; where floods are threatening.

Geographers, of course, find Landsat images a delight. They can now readily map hitherto uncharted remote regions, not only in their own country but virtually anywhere on Earth. Only small areas near the poles are lost to Landsat's all-seeing electronic eyes.

Weather View

But Landsat forms only part of the remote-sensing story. For the meteorologist, remote sensing means weather satellites, such as NOAA and GOES. They present us hour by hour, day by day with the familiar cloud-cover pictures we see on television weather forecasts.

Exciting things are also happening with remote sensing on the shuttle. Precision conventional photography is being carried out with the Large Format Camera and with the Metric Camera on Spacelab missions. The Shuttle Imaging Radar is producing highly detailed images at night as well as by day. The French (with SPOT) and the European Space Agency (with ERS) are also now becoming involved in remote sensing in a big way.

Remote sensing has been condemned by some countries as spying, and certainly they have a point. But Landsat images are available, not for the exclusive use of spies, but for use by anyone, in any country, for whatever purpose. Which is how it should be. Everyone on Earth should have the opportunity to marvel at the beauty of our home planet as revealed by the dazzling pictures from space.

A magnificent view of the full Earth taken by the European satellite Meteosat. It shows practically cloud-free skies over most of Europe and Africa, except for the Mediterranean region and tropical Africa. The picture is in simulated natural color. Meteosat normally takes cloud pictures in black and white.

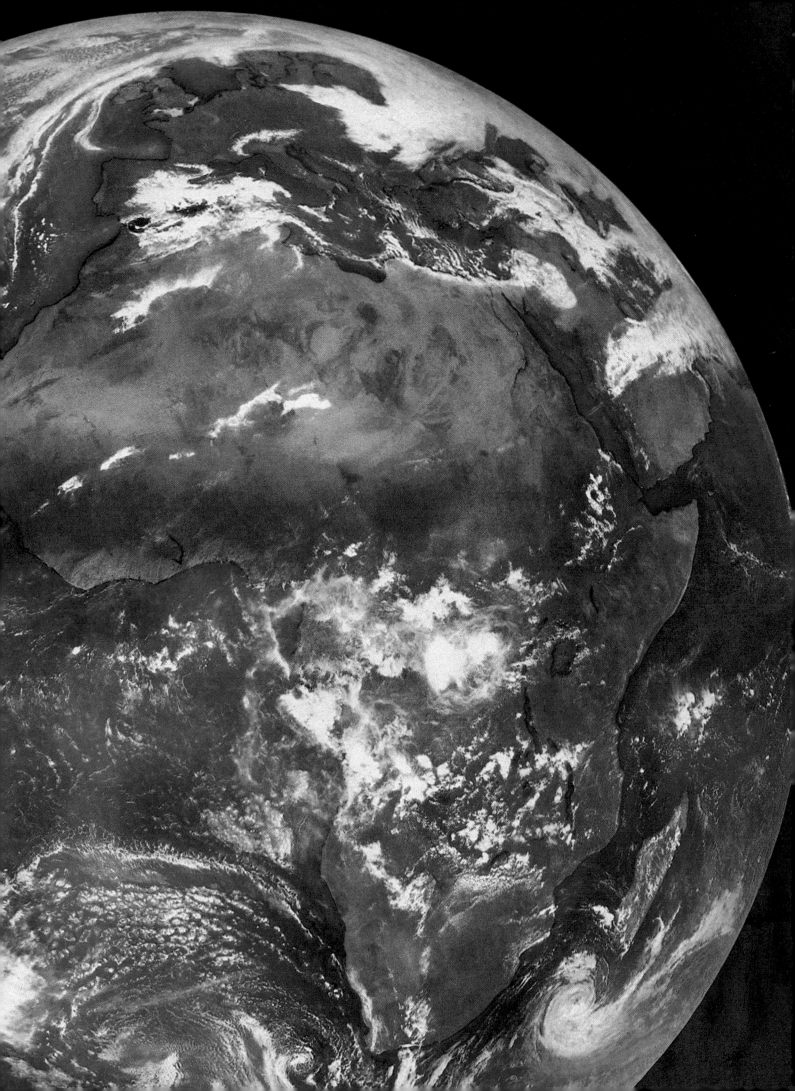

The Technology

Circling in orbit 435 miles (700 km) high, a satellite that represents the current technology of remote-sensing, turns its scanners on the western shores of Lake Erie. It is the fifth of the Landsat series of Earth-observing satellites, launched into orbit on March 1 1984. From its high vantage point it scans a 115 mile (185 km) square of the surface with its electronic eyes.

In less than half a minute it records electronically more than 30 million individual pieces of information about that square of land and water. In the blink of an eye it transmits this data to the Goddard Space Flight Center at Greenbelt, Maryland, just outside Washington DC. At Goddard the incoming data signals are recorded and processed for geometric and other corrections. Further processing results in a computer-compatible magnetic tape, which is then sent to the EROS Data Center at Sioux Falls, South Dakota.

At EROS, after further processing, the digital electronic data is fed into a film recorder, which uses a laser beam to produce a photographic image. The result is the picture you see on these pages, a spectacular view of Detroit, Windsor and Toledo and the surrounding countryside.

Of course, the countryside isn't really red! Landsat produces data which can be processed to give images in any color you like. In this picture the red represents vegetation in the fields, providing marked contrast to the blue-white of the urban areas. As we shall see later, a variety of computerized techniques is available to bring out particular surface features in the scanned area.

The Landsat Family

The Landsat story began in 1972. On July 23 of that year a butterfly-like satellite called the Earth Resources Technology Satellite 1 (ERTS-1) was launched into orbit. ERTS-1, later renamed Landsat 1, was joined in January 1975 by Landsat 2. And a third Landsat was launched in March 1978, two months after Landsat 1 had failed. All three satellites were of the same basic design as Nimbus, a highly successful weather satellite. Their butterfly-like appearance was due to their two 'wings' of solar panels. They were all launched from the Western Test Range, at Vandenberg Air Force Base in California, into near-polar orbits at a height of about 570 miles (920 km).

The Landsats carried two main instruments to view the Earth's surface, the RBV (Return Beam Vidicon) and the MSS (Multispectral Scanner). The RBV system used three television-type cameras, while the MSS used a novel oscillating mirror scanning system to image the ground. It was the MSSs that provided the bulk of the data. A MSS was also one of the two main sensors chosen for the next generation of Landsat satellites, Landsat 4 (July 1982) and 5 (March 1984). Of these, only Landsat 5 is now fully operational.

Landsat 5: The Spacecraft

This latest Landsat, which is identical to Landsat 4, is an adaptation of a standard NASA design, called the MSS (Multimission Modular Spacecraft). The basic design was also used for Solar Max, the satellite that shuttle astronauts so spectacularly repaired in orbit in April 1984. With its solar panels deployed, Landsat is 14 ft (4 meters) long and 7 ft (2 meters) across. Its 12.5 ft (3.7 meter) mast carries a 6 ft (1.8 meter) diameter dish antenna.

This Landsat 5 image of the western end of Lake Erie shows the state of the art in remote sending. Produced by Landsat's thematic mapper, it shows incredible detail of the landscape. At top center is the city and suburbs of Detroit. Across the Detroit River is the Canadian city of Windsor. The city in the south-west corner of Lake Erie is Toledo, in Ohio, at the mouth of the Maumee River.

Landsat 5 operates at a lower altitude than Landsats 1 to 3. It circles the Earth at a height of about 435 miles (700 km) every 100 minutes. The orbit is chosen so that it keeps pace with the Sun as the Earth is spinning – it is Sun-synchronous. As a result, Landsat always passes over a certain point on Earth at the same local time, about 9.30-10.00 am. It returns to the same point every 16 days. This contrasts with a return period of 18 days for Landsats 1 to 3. Because the angle of the Sun in Landsat images is always the same, differences in images taken at different times can be spotted more easily.

The Seasons

Landsat acquires much more information than an ordinary camera because of the way it looks at the Earth. It 'sees', not in ordinary light like we do, but in light of different wavelengths.

Now, most substances tend to appear different when viewed in light of different wavelengths of the spectrum. We say that they have different spectral 'signatures'. Using Landsat data, we can more easily spot these signatures and thereby identify surface features which may go unnoticed in ordinary (white) light.

Two sensors are used by Landsat 5, the Multispectral Scanner (MSS) and the Thematic Mapper (TM). The MSS scans the Earth at four wavelengths, or more accurately in four wavebands, which each cover a range of wavelengths. One band is in the visible green part of the spectrum; one is in the visible red; and two are in the invisible near-infrared. The thematic mapper can scan in three additional wavebands – one more in the green and two in the infrared. The bands are chosen so as to bring out contrasts in surface features. For example, the first band in the green shows up differences between deciduous and coniferous forests and emphasizes coastal features, such as shoals, reefs and sediment-laden waters. The red band emphasizes differences in plant species. The middle infrared band can distinguish between snow and cloud.

A Hughes technician checking out Landsat's thematic mapper before it is mounted on the spacecraft. It is the most sensitive of Landsat's instruments and gives the highest resolution images. The scanning apparatus is inside the circular opening. On the left of the picture is the electronics module, at the front of which is a set of louvers. These open or close as necessary to keep the module at optimum working temperature.

Both the MSS and the TM use an oscillating mirror device to scan the surface continuously in a succession of 115 mile (185 km) swaths, from right to left (west to east) as Landsat travels south. The mirror directs the light reflected from the surface through filters onto detectors for each waveband.

The smallest surface detail the MSS can resolve is an area 270 ft (82 m) square. This forms the basic picture element, or pixel, of the MSS image system. The TM, however, has much higher resolution. It generates images with pixels only 98 ft (30 m) square. Hence it can see much more detail than the MSS.

Relaying and Distributing the Data

Landsat 5 can transmit its MSS and TM data to Earth in a variety of ways. If it is within line of sight of a Landsat ground station such as Goddard, then it can transmit the data to it directly. If it is out of sight of a ground station, it may be within sight of a TDRS (Tracking and Data Relay Satellite). If so, it can transmit data (via its dish antenna) to the TDRS, which then relays it to ground station at White Sands, New Mexico. From there the data goes to Goddard via a domestic communications satellite. If there is no satellite or ground station within range, then Landsat stores the scanning data on tape recorders, to be played back when convenient.

The Goddard Space Flight Center at Greenbelt, Maryland, is one of three main Landsat receiving stations in the United States. The others

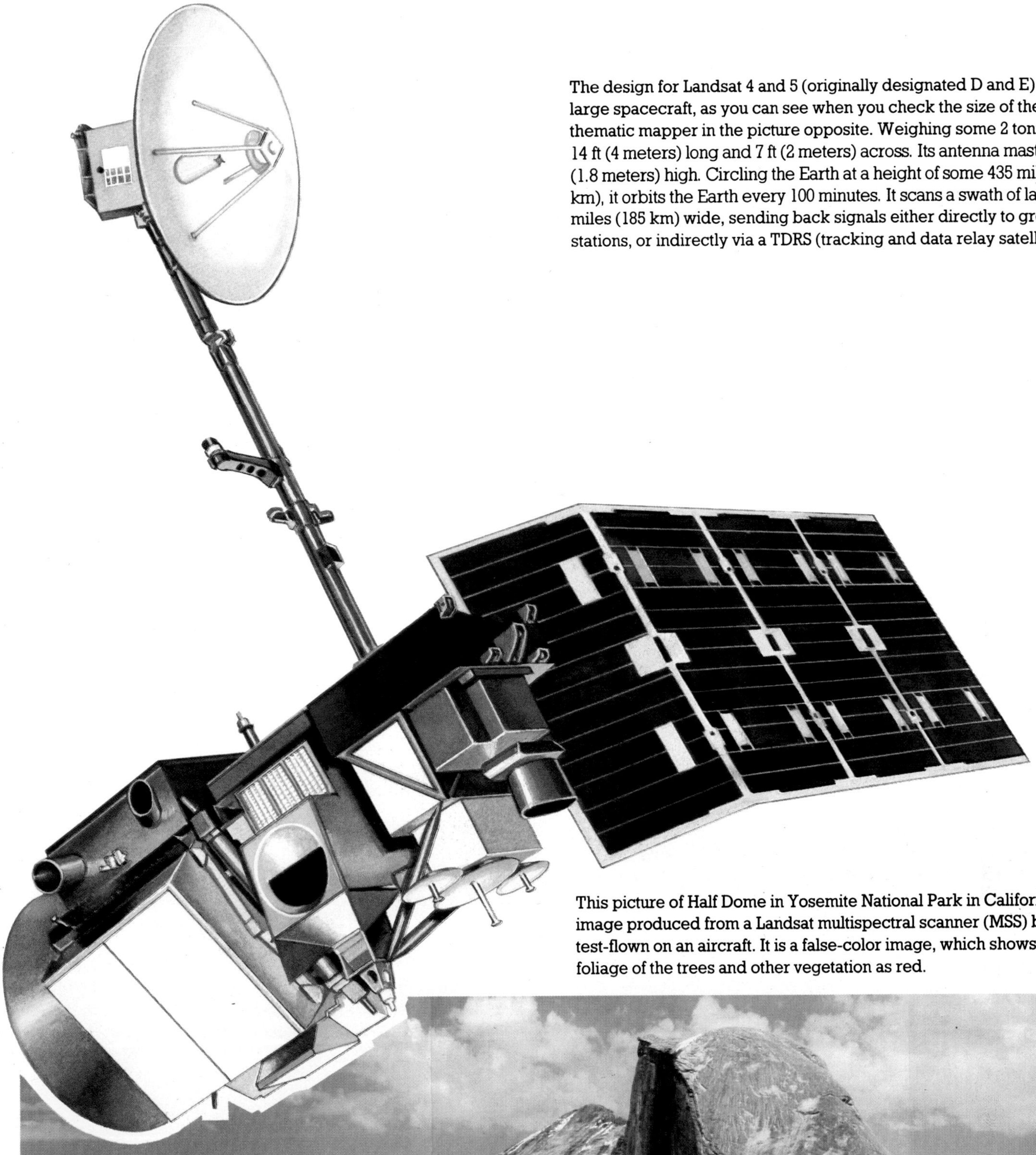

The design for Landsat 4 and 5 (originally designated D and E). It is a large spacecraft, as you can see when you check the size of the thematic mapper in the picture opposite. Weighing some 2 tonnes, it is 14 ft (4 meters) long and 7 ft (2 meters) across. Its antenna mast is 6 ft (1.8 meters) high. Circling the Earth at a height of some 435 miles (700 km), it orbits the Earth every 100 minutes. It scans a swath of land 115 miles (185 km) wide, sending back signals either directly to ground stations, or indirectly via a TDRS (tracking and data relay satellite).

This picture of Half Dome in Yosemite National Park in California is an image produced from a Landsat multispectral scanner (MSS) being test-flown on an aircraft. It is a false-color image, which shows the foliage of the trees and other vegetation as red.

are at Goldstone, California; and Fairbanks, Alaska. There are several other Landsat receiving stations located throughout the world. In Europe there are two, at Kiruna in Sweden and Fucino in Italy. Data received through these stations is distributed throughout Europe by a network called Earthnet from a center at Frascati in Italy. There are also Landsat receiving stations in Australia, Canada, Brazil, Argentina, South Africa, and the Far East.

EROS Data Center

The overall responsibility for Landsat operations now rests with NOAA, the National Oceanic and Atmospheric Administration. The EROS Data Center in Sioux Falls is operated by NOAA as a processing and research facility for Landsat imagery, and the prime distribution center in the United States. (EROS stands for Earth Resources Observation Systems.)

The EROS Data Center also distributes imagery acquired on the Gemini, Skylab and Apollo missions. In addition it markets detailed aerial photographs covering the United States, in black and white, ordinary color, and false-color infrared. Some have been taken as part of NASA's Earth Resources Aircraft Program; others for the National High-Altitude Photography Program (NHAP). NASA aerial photographs were taken at various altitudes, from a few thousand feet to more than 11 miles (18 km). The NHAP photographs were taken from a standard altitude of 40,000 ft (12,000 meters).

Landsat Images

Landsat sends back information about the Earth's surface in the form of electronic digital data. This represents the output from the individual detectors for the four wavebands of the MSS and the seven wavebands of the TM. The data relating to each waveband is separated and processed to form an image, which can then be 'written' on film. You may notice that a Landsat image is not square, like a photograph. It is a parellelogram, because the sides are parallel to the orbital track of the satellite across the Earth's surface. Each side of the standard Landsat image represents a distance on the ground of 115 miles (185 km).

The image made from a single waveband is typically printed in black and white. So MSS data for a Landsat scene would yield a set of four black-and-white images, displaying differences in the appearance of the same area at green, red and near-infrared wavelengths.

For most purposes the differences in surface characteristics became more evident when the individual waveband data are combined into a false-color composite. One way of producing false-color composites is to expose three of the black-and-white waveband images through filters onto color film. The colors produced, however, are false – not true to life. Healthy vegetation appears bright red, not green; urban areas appear blue or blue-gray; clear water appears black, sediment-laden water powder blue. This system of producing composites from black-and-white film, however, has been largely superseded. Nowadays false-color images are created directly from the original digital data, and are therefore of much better quality.

Image Processing

The data outputted from a Landsat receiver center, such as Goddard, has already been processed to a certain extent. But for most user applications, the data is still considered 'raw' and requires further processing by computer. Several processes are now routinely carried out.

The raw Landsat data has already been corrected for such things as the curvature of the Earth and satellite attitude errors. But the image is still distorted as far as a standard map is concerned. A process called 'geometric transformation' brings the image into line with the map.

'Density slicing' is a technique that brings out contrasts in

Landsat data is received from the spacecraft in electronic digital form. It is then computer-processed into an image. Here a researcher at EROS Data Center near Sioux Falls, South Dakota, is carrying out a digital analysis on an image of the Hawaiian island of Oahu.

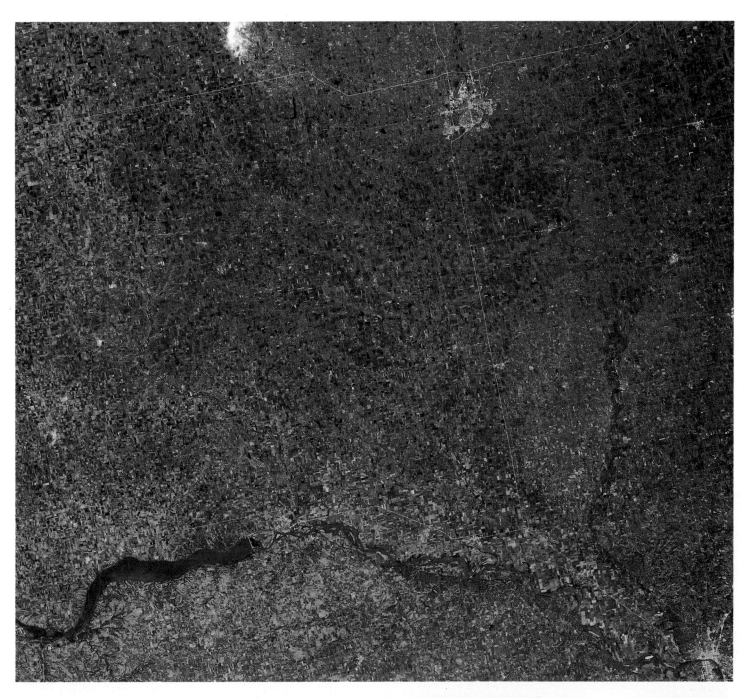

Landsat's thematic mapper imaged this mainly agricultural region of the south-east corner of South Dakota. The river near the bottom of the picture is the Missouri, which marks the state line with Nebraska. Notice on the left, the dam across the river (the Gavins Point dam), containing the Lewis and Clark Lake. The city near the top of the picture is Sioux Falls, home of the EROS Data Center. Note how clearly the airport runways stand out.

The EROS Data Center north-east of Sioux Falls. The building shown here is the 120,000 square-ft (11,200 square-meter) Karl E. Mundt Federal Building. The heart of the Center is a powerful computer complex, which controls a data base of over six million images and photographs.

continuously changing values (say, depths of water). Different false-colors are assigned to certain ranges of values (1-5, 5-10 fathoms, for example). The resulting image makes it easier for the eye to spot essential differences.

Another technique uses a 'target signature' for rapid location of particular surface features. First you determine the spectral signature of a desired feature, say a particular crop, then you can instruct the computer to highlight in false color all the areas in the image with this signature.

Shuttle Photography and Images
Landsat produces images of the Earth's surface that are not true to life. To see what the Earth really looks like, we must turn to photographs taken by the astronauts, with ordinary cameras, on ordinary color film. Today, the shuttle astronauts snap away on every mission, continuing the work of the pioneer space photographers on the Gemini, Apollo and Skylab missions.

The astronauts generally use Hasselblad cameras and 70 mm film to take photographs. These are all taken, of course, through the shuttle's windows, which are of high optical quality. The colors in shuttle

NASA has an airborne Earth resources program as well as a space-based one. This stunning infrared image of Niagara Falls was taken from a height of some 2500 ft (760 meters). The spectacular Canadian, or Horseshoe Falls are on the right; the American Falls are on the left. Note how vegetation and foliage shows up as shades of red. Landsat instruments record images at several infrared wavelengths.

photographs are not as vivid as might be expected. The greens of vegetation, for example, tend to come out as bluish-gray. This is the result of the scattering of light in the Earth's atmosphere.

The shuttle also acts as carrier for more advanced space cameras and other remote-sensing equipment. On the 41-G mission in October 1984, for example, the Large Format Camera (LFC) made its space début for test purposes and calibration. It is capable of giving a ground resolution of about 70 ft (21 meters), which compares with 82 ft (30 meters) with Landsat's thematic mapper.

Flying on the 41-G mission, too, was the second Shuttle Imaging Radar (SIR). Like the Large Format Camera, it is carried in the shuttle orbiter's payload bay which is always open to space. The SIR works like any radar, by transmitting pulses of microwaves and detecting their echoes. But unlike ordinary radar it can transmit pulses to strike the surface at different angles. The strength of the echoes depends on the nature of the surface. By computer processing the echoes, an image of the surface can be built up.

Because microwaves are used, this image can be obtained at any time, day or night, and in all weather conditions. This is an improvement over Landsat, which uses reflected sunlight and requires daylight cloud-free conditions for good imagery.

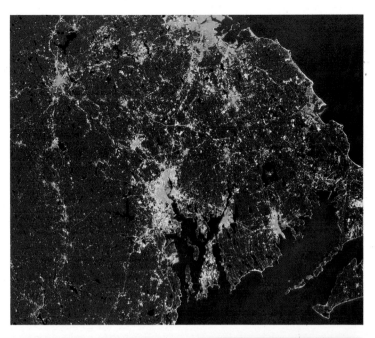

This full-frame image of New England was taken by a Landsat multispectral scanner (MSS). The false colors contrast the urban areas (blue-white) with the countryside (red). Inland waters are black. At top center is Boston, Massachusetts, at center is Providence, Rhode Island. The resolution of the image is not brilliant.

A closer view of Boston, showing the high resolution possible from the thematic mapper. The highways, for example, show up clearly, as do highway intersections. Again the colors are false, although they have been chosen to show up the countryside in green.

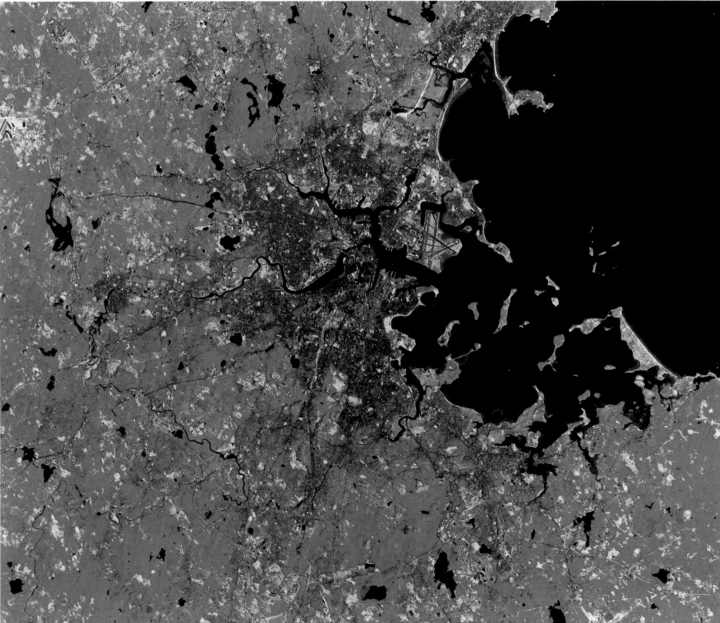

Standing on a pillar of flame, smoke and steam, a space shuttle blasts off from the launch pad at the Kennedy Space Center in Florida. Dominating the scene is the skyscraper-tall Vehicle Assembly Building, in which the shuttle stack is assembled. The shuttle is becoming more and more involved in remote sensing through the shuttle imaging radar (SIR) and large format camera (LFC) programs.

The Kennedy space port in this astronaut's view of Cape Canaveral and Merritt Island. The Vehicle Assembly Building and the two shuttle launch pads are clearly visible.

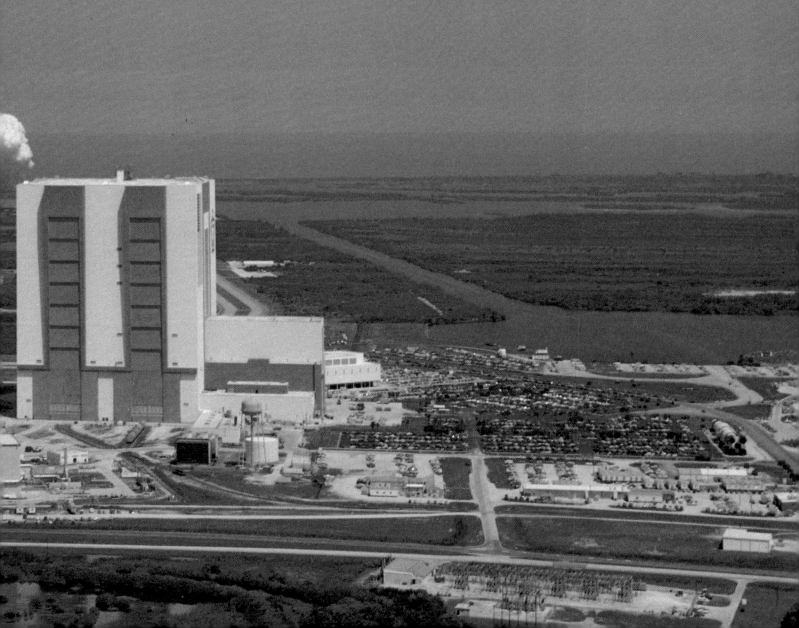

Skylab astronauts snapped this picture of the space station before starting a record-breaking 59-day mission in July 1973. Far below the sun glints on the mighty Amazon River in Brazil. Much of the on-board photography of Skylab was excellent. A remote-sensing camera package took multispectral images comparable in quality to those now being obtained from Landsat's thematic mapper.

Some of the most exciting sensing work on the shuttle is done by the shuttle imaging radar (SIR). This instrument operates from inside the payload bay. It scans the ground in narrow strips, and the images are generally shown in black and white. Here an image taken of part of the Sahara desert is superimposed on one obtained from Landsat. It shows details of the rocky surface underlying the covering of sand.

Shuttle astronauts have taken many outstanding true color photographs of the Earth with hand-held cameras. This one shows the vast Nile Delta in Egypt and the Mediterranean. Cairo is directly above the orbiter's tail. To the right of the port engine pod is the Great Bitter Lake. Leading from it is the Suez Canal, which meets the Mediterranean at Port Said.

A broader view of the Earth's surface than that provided by a single Landsat image can be obtained by combining individual images into a mosaic. This false-color photomosaic of the contiguous United States was produced from 569 standard Landsat images. The processing was done by General Electric. Even at this scale such details as the outflow from the Mississippi delta show up.

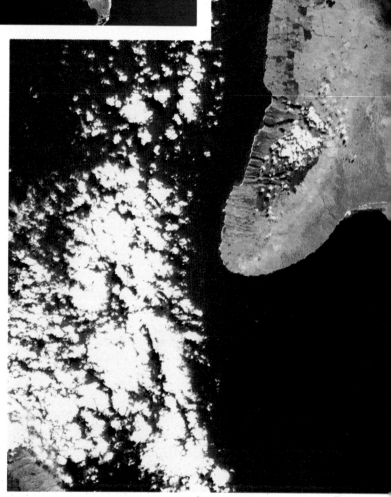

This beautiful photomosaic of Hawaii shows the island in simulated natural color. At the center of the island the massive Mauna Loa volcano is surrounded on all sides by lava flows. It is about 120 ft (36 meters) lower than Mauna Kea to the left, which soars to 13,800 ft (4200 meters). Above Mauna Loa is the perennially active Kilauea.

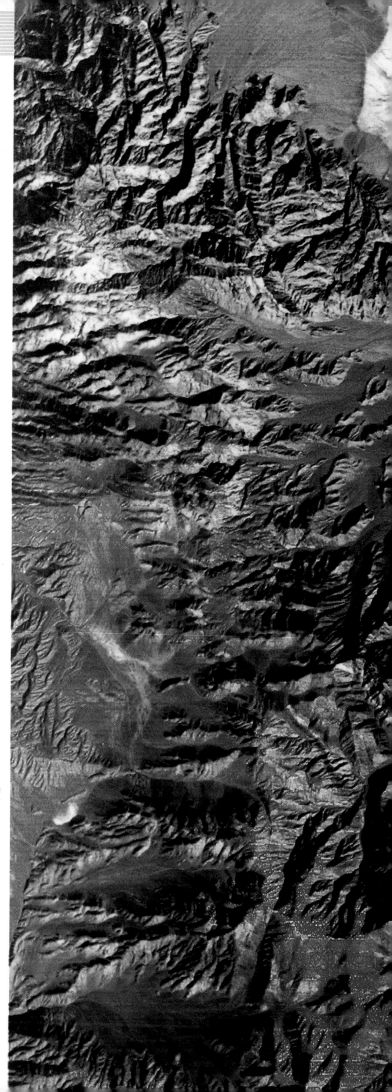

The Land

You would need few guesses to pick out two groups of people who have perhaps benefited the most from remote-sensing. They are cartographers – scientists who make maps; and geologists – scientists concerned with the study of rocks, minerals and of the structure of the Earth's surface and the changes that take place in it.

Before Landsat became operational, map making was a painstaking and laborious process. The making of geological maps was even worse, requiring detailed in-the-field investigation and sampling as well as actual surveys. In remote regions of the world this was not possible, and consequently there were huge gaps in geological knowledge. These gaps no longer exist, for Landsat can image virtually the whole of the Earth's surface in just 16 days (Landsat 5).

Mapping Egypt

Cartographers and geologists can now map anywhere in the world with complete accuracy, quickly and economically. For example, in the 1970s, Egypt used Landsat data to produce a detailed geological map of the the country for about $15 million in about 5 years. Had conventional mapping techniques been employed, it would have taken twice as long and cost twice as much, and the maps would have contained less than half the detail.

The standard Landsat image shows up most ground features in remarkable detail. And further detail can be squeezed out by sympathetic computer processing. This is known as image enhancement. Look at the detail in the picture of Death Valley shown here. It shows the mountain structure with great clarity and the courses of the mountain streams that are washing sediment into the valley, creating classic 'alluvial fans'. The red on the valley floor highlights deposits of silt there.

The remoteness of Landsat's view of the Earth brings with it distinct advantages. The images clearly show up regional features that larger-scale aerial photography may miss. The whole sweep of intercontinental mountain ranges can be appreciated, and fault lines traced in their entirety. For residents of California, fault lines are of particular interest. The San Francisco Bay area is riddled with them, the most notorious being the San Andreas Fault. Here, as in many faults regions, there is an ever-present threat of earthquakes.

Searching Underground

Faults however have their good side. They are often areas in which mineral deposits form. Mineral deposits and oil are often associated with other geological structures, such as folds and domes. Landsat can detect these too. Mineral deposits may reveal themselves as discolorations of the surrounding rocks, which may be invisible to the eye but visible to Landsat's multispectral scanners. In some areas where mineral deposits are located underground, the surface vegetation is affected in a way that only Landsat can detect. It is not surprising that the oil and mining industries are the biggest purchasers of Landsat data.

You don't have to be a scientist or a prospector though to appreciate the multicolored views of the Earth's surface that Landsat produces. For us all, Landsat images bring the world into vivid focus. We can see how

Death Valley in south-east California, the hottest and driest region in North America, where temperatures have been known to soar to 57°C. This image was produced by Landsat 4's thematic mapper, and color coded so as to enhance the geological structure of the mountains bordering the Valley, the Amargosa (on the right) and the Panamint Ranges. They soar to some 6500 ft (2000 meters), while Death Valley plummets to 282 ft (86 meters) below sea level, the lowest point in the Western hemisphere.

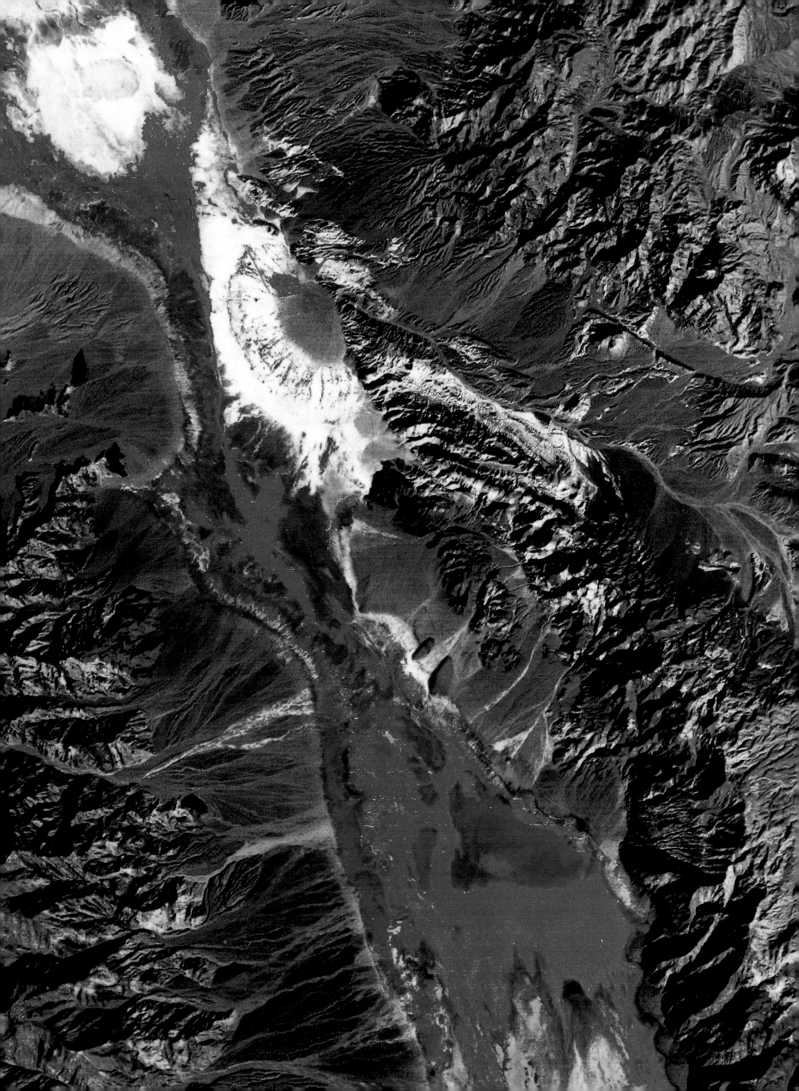

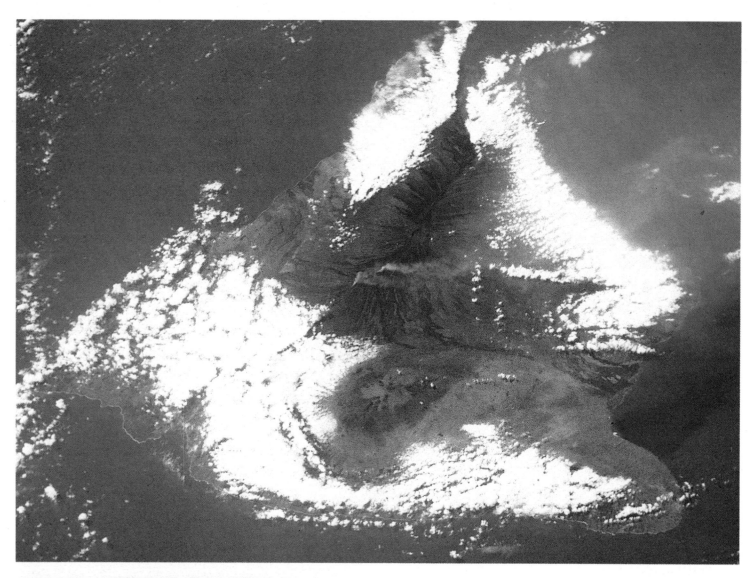

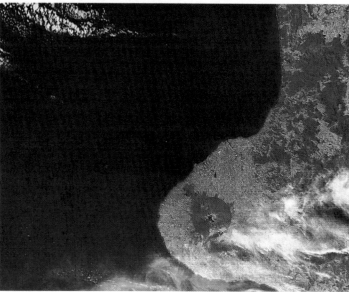

the rivers have carved their way through the landscape, and the devastation they can cause when they flood. We can follow the lava flow from erupting volcanoes, which hint at seething activity beneath the surface. We can see where the surface has wrinkled under inexorable pressures, and created lofty mountain ranges. We can venture, safely, to some of the remotest, coldest, and hottest places on Earth, thanks to Landsat.

▲

Fumes and steam rise from a river of molten lava coming down the slopes of Mauna Loa volcano in April 1984. This photograph, looking south over the island, was snapped by astronauts on shuttle mission 41-C. Below Mauna Loa in the picture is Mauna Kea, a volcano which has not erupted for several thousand years. Hidden beneath the clouds on the left of the picture is Kilauea volcano, also in eruption at the time. Compare this photograph with the Hawaii mosaic on page 21.

▲

A perfectly circular structure shows the extent of lava flows from Mt Egmont on the west coast of the North Island of New Zealand. This dormant volcano, which last erupted about 300 years ago, has an almost perfectly shaped volcanic cone. This is a conventional MSS Landsat image.

One of the excellent infrared photographs taken from Skylab in 1973 ▶ by the Earth-Resources Experiment Package. It shows an active Mt Etna on the east coast of the Mediterranean island of Sicily. The extent of lava flows from previous eruptions is clearly seen. The lava from the most recent eruption appear darkest. Just along the coast from the 10,960-ft (3340-meter) high mountain is the town of Catania.

25

San Francisco Bay, as pictured from 435 miles (700 km) high by Landsat 4's thematic mapper. The densely populated area around the Bay is hemmed in by low mountains, rising at the top of the picture to 3850 ft (1173 meters) at Mt Diablo. Geologically the most interesting feature, however, is the infamous San Andreas fault, which runs south-east from San Francisco. It can readily be traced in the image, along the San Andreas reservoir and Crystal Springs Lakes, alongside Interstate Highway 280.

The shuttle imaging radar produced this image of the rock structure of the high plateau of northern Peru. Subtle color coding by computer has resulted in a geologically very informative picture. Traversing the image is the Maranon River, a major tributary of the Amazon.

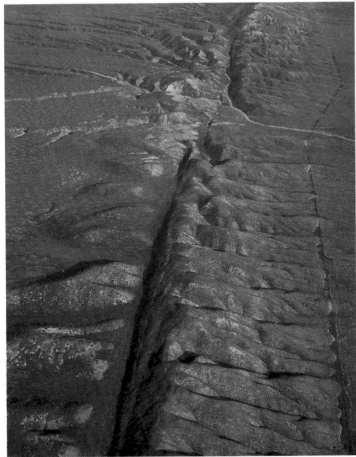

The devastation caused by San Francisco's massive earthquake on 18 April 1906. The quake and the fires it started wiped out four square miles (10 square km) of the city, killing as many as 700 people. It was caused by sudden movement along the San Andreas fault (left) marking a region of the Earth's surface where adjacent crustal 'plates' are rubbing together. A similar disaster could occur again at any time.

Movement of the Earth's crust also accounted for the world's highest mountain range, the Himalayas. This Landsat MSS image shows this desolate region, well named 'the roof of the world'. Highest mountain Everest (29,028 ft, 8848 meters) lies in the range near the top left of the picture on the border of China (north) and Nepal. It is a region of perpetual snows.

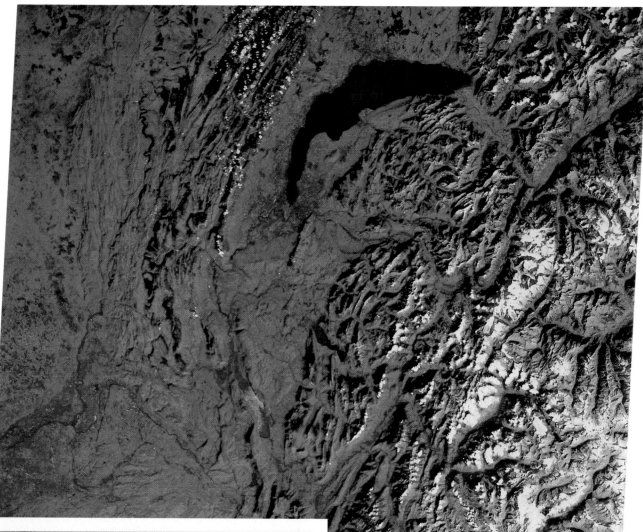

Dominating this autumn Landsat MSS image is the crescent shaped Lake Geneva. It is sandwiched between the Jura Mountains on the left and the Alps. Highest peak in the Alps, Mt Blanc (15,780 ft, 4810 meters) is located to the south-east of the Lake under snow cover. Snow has not yet come to much of this mountainous region, which shows up mainly red-orange in color because of extensive vegetation cover. The blue-gray color shows areas above the timberline not yet covered with snow.

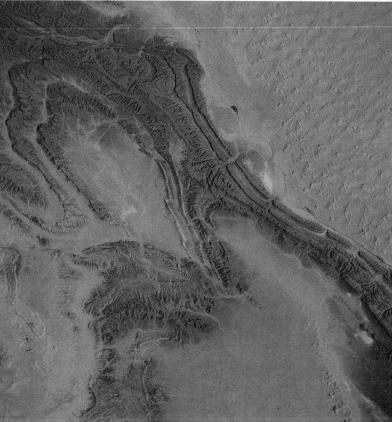

Conventional orbital photography shows fascinating glimpses of normally inaccessible areas of the Earth, as here in Algeria. At the upper right are the desert sands of the Grand Erg Occidental. Notice the dune patterns. The desert is bounded here by the low fold mountains of the Raoui Range.

Gas being burnt off at an oil rig in the Middle East. The gas is pumped from the wells with the oil and must be removed before the oil is piped to storage tanks.

Another desert scene (Landsat MSS), this time showing a region bordering the Persian Gulf. The island is Bahrain. This part of the Middle East has some of the world's most productive oilfields. And this image shows more than a dozen wells in full production. You can see the smoke and sometimes the flames coming from the gas being burned at the rigs.

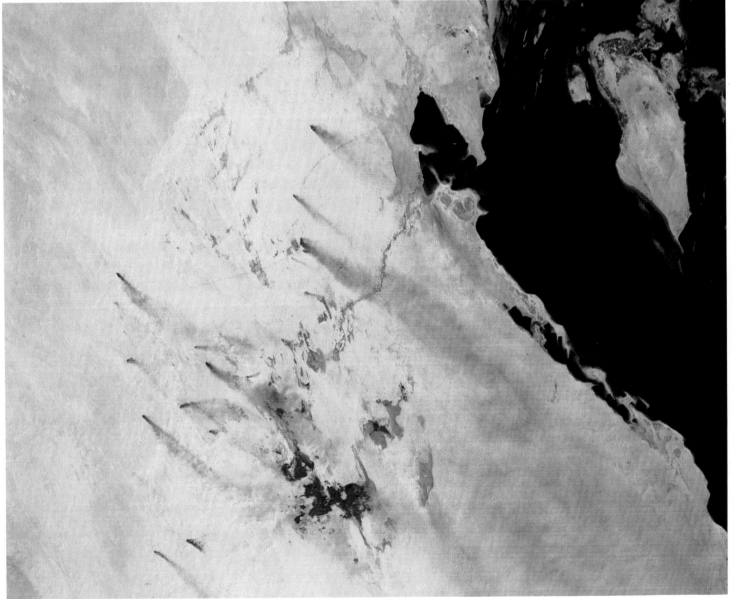

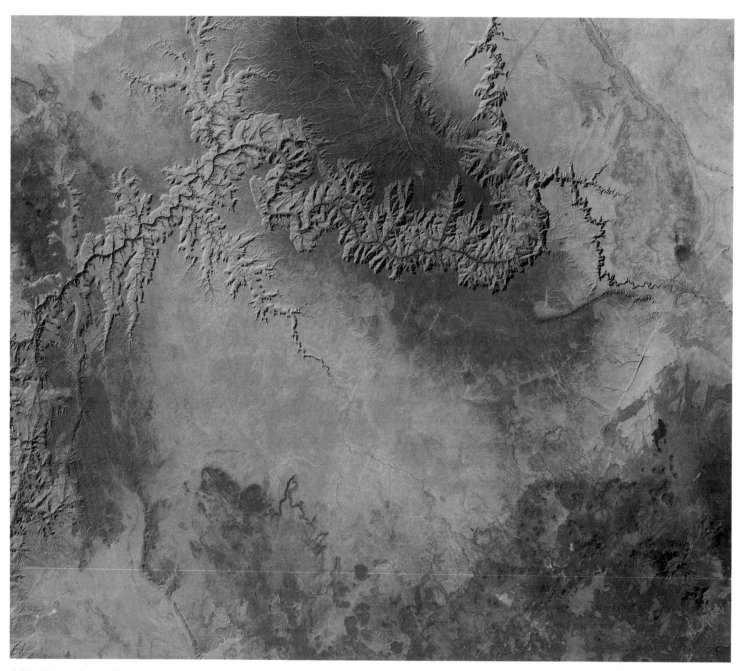

Orbital view of one of the greatest natural wonders of the world, the Grand Canyon in Arizona. This great gash in the Earth's surface up to a mile (1.6 km) deep, was made by the Colorado River cutting through the rocks over a period of hundreds of millions of years. Other interesting features of this image (Landsat MSS) is the Kaibab Plateau north of the Canyon and the volcanic peak bottom right. This is Humphrey's Peak, at 12,670 ft (3861 meters) the highest point in Arizona. Just south of it is the city of Flagstaff.

This photograph of the Grand Canyon shows the strata exposed as the Colorado River cut into the rock. It was taken from the Bright Angel Trail.

Shuttle astronauts photographed this fascinating circular feature in western Mauritania in West Africa. Although it looks man-made it is actually caused by wind erosion. Known as a Richat structure, it is a 1000 ft (300 meter) deep hole in the ground that rises in steep concentric ridges. At the top it measures 25 miles (40 km) across. Just visible on the extreme left is a similar smaller feature, called the Semsiyyat dome.

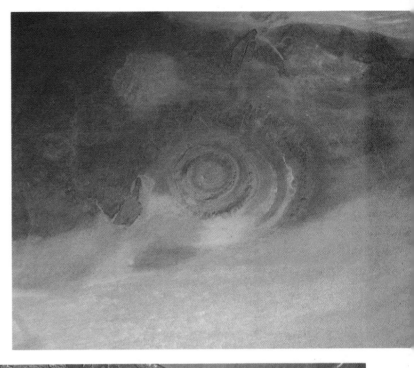

The Mississippi River is also slowly eroding the landscape, though not as spectacularly as the Colorado. After travelling for some 3700 miles (5955 km) from Minnesota, 'Old Man River' reaches the sea just south of New Orleans. As this Landsat MSS image shows, it carries with it a lot of sediment, which is continually enlarging the delta area.

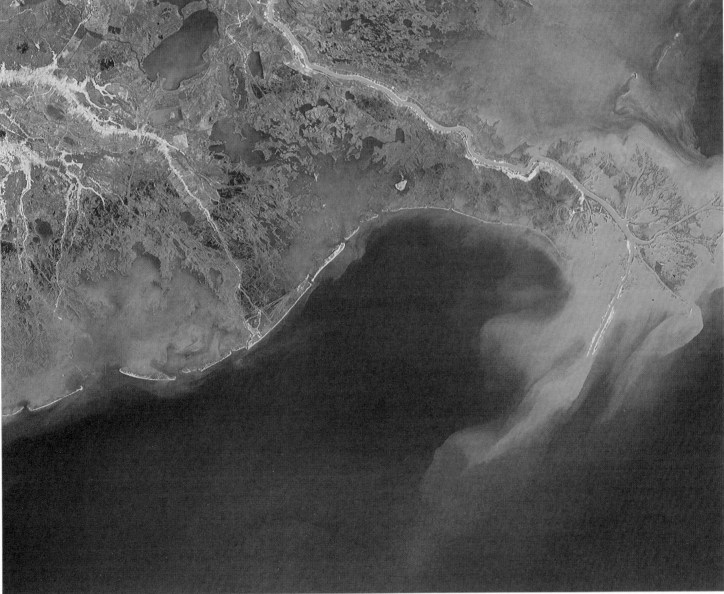

Land Use

Looking down on the Earth from space, Landsat records evidence of the hand of Man in nearly every image it takes. As it passes over the Great Plains region in the heartland of the United States, for example, the near-perfect geometry of the square north-south, east-west field pattern hits its electronic eyes. In most US cities the strict grid pattern is also adhered to. It could only be man-made. Natural features are seldom straight, nor do they align themselves with the compass points.

The hands of Man reveals itself in many other ways besides. In images of the Sahara Desert, patterns of dark circular dots show up, contrasting with the surrounding sandy desert. They are also too regular to be anything but man-made – they are in fact center-pivot irrigation schemes. In the great snow 'desert' of North Alaska, flames and plumes of smoke mark the location of rigs where oil engineers bring the precious 'black gold' to the surface from subterranean wells.

Invaluable Knowledge

Landsat images record all the multifarious activities of mankind, the crops we grow, the forests we chop down, the lakes we dam, the land we mine for minerals, the cities we build, the pollution we cause. All in all, they provide an invaluable means of monitoring land use.

An up-to-date picture of land use such as Landsat can provide, is becoming increasingly necessary as town and country planners get to grips with the problems of an expanding population, which requires space for living and an adequate food supply. Intelligent planning will ensure that the best possible use is made of the available resources.

Filling in the Details

In both town and country, Landsat can detect subtle differences in ground features, that make land classification possible. It can distinguish their characteristic spectral signatures. So in urban areas it can spot different levels of habitation, such as a central business district, characterized by high-density building; sparse residential areas with moderate growth of trees; denser residential areas with grass cover; and so on.

However, it is in the country, in agricultural applications, that Landsat data is being put to best use. Even in technologically advanced countries like the United States, details of crop acreages and crop yields were until recently usually inaccurate, out of date or incomplete. Using Landsat data, however, the situation has been greatly improved, allowing more accurate forward planning. Agricultural practice in developing countries could be revolutionized by applying Landsat data.

Watching the Crops

The precision with which this remarkable spacecraft can follow the cropping cycle is uncanny. On a standard false-color composite image, unplanted fields show up as blue or shades of brown, depending on the soil. The growing crops gradually change color (in the images) from pale pink to bright red as they mature. Their spectral signature also changes if they suffer 'stress' of any kind, such as disease, insect attack, frost, hail or drought.

All this can be readily monitored by Landsat, which is also capable of distinguishing between different crops with a better than 90 per cent

The River Thames winds lazily through the center of London in this Landsat 4 thematic mapper image. The image has been color-coded to show up the various parks and open spaces in Britain's capital city. Prominent to the north of the Thames is the squarish Hyde Park, containing the Serpentine Lake. In the south-east, Hyde Park joins with Green Park and St James's Park, wherein lies Buckingham Palace.

accuracy. It can distinguish, for example, between field corn and pop corn, sunflower and alfalfa, grown in adjacent fields. It can also recognize different kinds of standing timber. Evergreen conifers appear dark red in standard composites and remain that way throughout the growing season, whereas deciduous trees change from pink to red to brown as the season progresses.

This Landstat thematic mapper image shows the south- west corner of Minnesota. The color coding shows sharp contrast between the patchwork of fields with growing crops (red) and the blue-gray built-up areas. Plowed fields also show up blue-gray because they have a similar spectral signature to concrete.

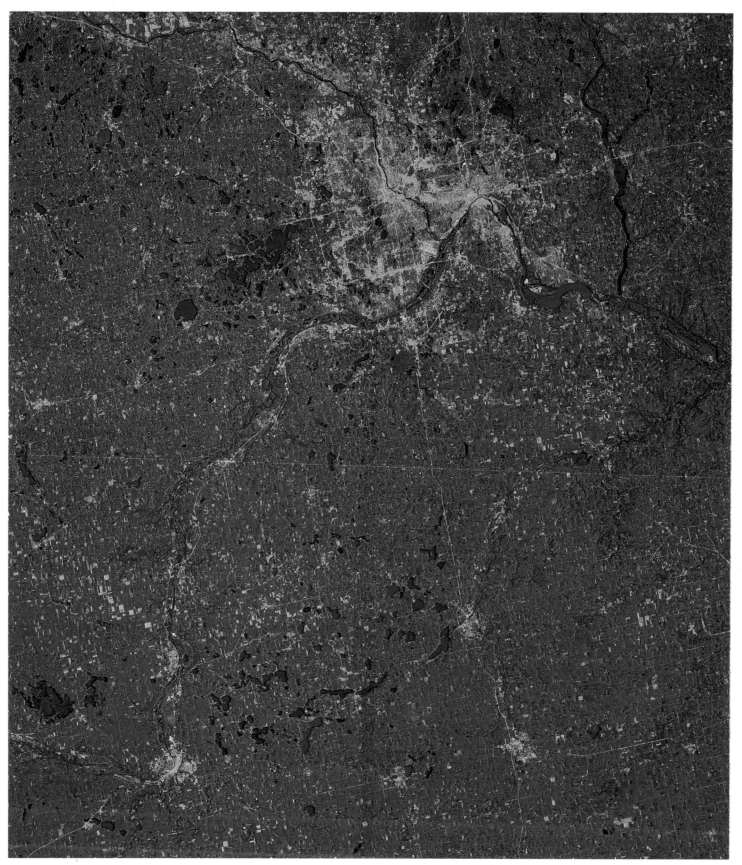

In an early experiment with crop recognition from space, Apollo 9 photographs from orbit (above) and aerial photographs (below) were taken of a test site at Mesa, Arizona, on the same date (March 12, 1969). False colors were given to the space image to provide contrast between different stages of growth of different crops. The aerial shot is an infrared photograph.

Landsat images now provide agriculturists with a ready method of identifying crops and assessing their health and probable yield. They can also estimate the extent of the damage caused to the crops by frost, flood, fire and other natural disasters. This Landsat MSS image has been computer processed to bring out better definition in the crop pattern in the San Joaquin Valey in California.

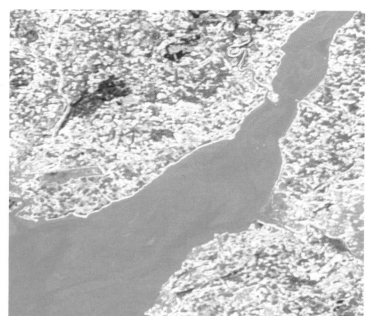

Because Landsat data are received in digital electronic form, they readily lend themselves to a variety of computer-processing techniques. Some of them are shown in this series of images of England's Bristol Channel region, generated from the same Landsat data. The technique chosen in a particular case will depend on what kind of information is required. The above picture shows a basic, or 'raw' image produced from the data with no particular application in mind.

Here the image has been 'contrast stretched'. Differences between shades of color have been enhanced. This can be done with monochrome (black-and-white) images from a single spectral band. A similar technique is used to highlight details in shuttle imaging radar pictures.

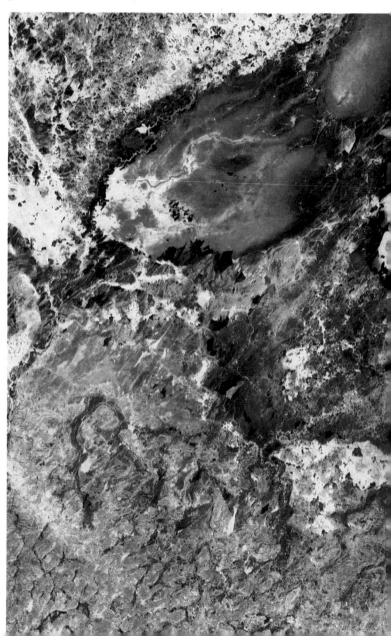

This image of the Scottish highlands illustrates well the versatility of computer-processing techniques. The various categories of land use have been separately color-coded for immediate recognition. It would be economically impossible to carry out such land classification in any other way.

Key

Blue = water	Green = woodland
Yellow = agriculture	Magenta = rough grass
Beige = heath/moorland	Red = urban
Black = unclassified	

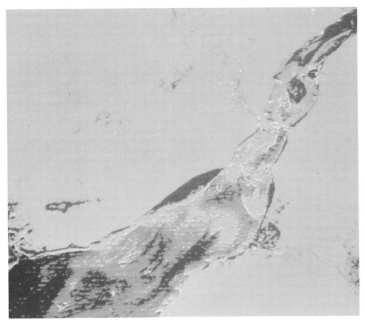

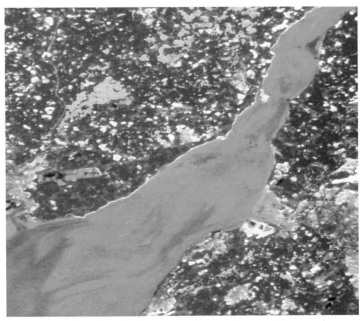

This image has been produced by 'density slicing'. In a normal image the range of tones is continuous, and it is difficult for the eye to spot differences. In density slicing, a different color is assigned to specific ranges of tones, which allows differences to be more easily spotted. This technique is used, for example, in showing water depths.

Another very handy technique uses a 'target signature' for classification. This is a spectral 'fingerprint' identifying a particular feature, such as pine forest. Once this signature is known, the processing computer can be instructed to print out areas of the image having this signature in false color, as has been done here in yellow.

Landsat imagery is particularly valuable for surveying and assessing land use in remote areas of the world with poor ground communications. Precision computer processing can yield an abundance of detail, as evidenced by this image of part of the flood region of the Upper Nile Basin in the southern Sudan. The prominent red areas show wet grassland subject to prolonged flooding, which become the main grazing lands in the dry season. White shows areas of intensive cultivation. Blue shows where overgrazing has occurred. Black shows areas of recent burning. Dark green represents seasonally wet clay grasslands.

This whole-frame Landsat thematic mapper image of the Chesapeake
Bay and Potomac River region of the eastern United States sums up the
benefits of satellite imagery to the map-maker much more eloquently
than words. Even at this scale the detail is startling. Further processing
can enhance particular features or areas of interest. The two major
cities in the picture are Baltimore to the north and Washington, DC.

Zeroing-in still further on Washington we have one of the most recent aerial photographs of the city, taken at 40,000 ft (12,000 meters) as part of the National High Altitude Photography program (NHAP). Taken on infrared film, it shows vegetation as red. It is interesting to compare the detail available in the three images on these two pages.

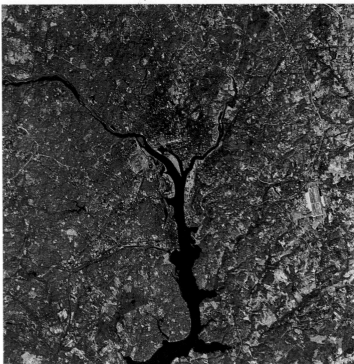

This image has been produced from the same Landsat data as the Chesapeake Bay image. Here we have zeroed-in on Washington and the Potomac River, and the image has been printed in simulated natural color. Cultural details are clearly visible. You can even see the shadow cast by the 555 ft (169 meter) high Washington Monument!

There can be few photographs of the San Francisco Bay area more dramatic than this one, a high-altitude aerial picture taken in infrared at an oblique angle. The effect is heightened by the horizon, where the atmosphere merges into the blackness of space. This perspective highlights certain features, such as the hills of the San Diablo Range beyond the Bay and even Twin Peaks in the heart of San Francisco. But distances are difficult to judge.

By contrast Landsat scanned the Bay area from vertically overhead, producing much less distortion. This MSS image was created using 'old technology', being a composite produced from a combination of dyed images made from black and white transparencies of different spectral bands. Landsat images are now usually created directly onto photographic film via computer.

This third view of San Francisco Bay is the oldest. It was taken by Skylab astronauts in 1973. It shows one of the most characteristic weather features of the area, banks of low cloud and fog rolling in from the Pacific to blanket 'everyone's favorite city'. This phenomenon of chilling summer fog occurs when warm moist sea air comes into contact with cold water welling up from the seabed along the coast. Skylab Earth-resource photographs like this showed what benefits satellite imagery could bring.

This infrared aerial photograph of central New Orleans reveals what the 'white dot' is in the Landsat picture. It is the famous Superdome, the largest indoor sports stadium in the world. Completed in 1975, it is 680 ft (208 meters) in diameter, and covers 13 acres (5.3 hectares). To the north is City Park, also visible in the Landsat picture, and Audubon Park to the west.

Lake Pontchartrain and below it New Orleans dominate this Landsat thematic mapper image of south-east Louisiana. Snaking through New Orleans is the Mississippi River, nearly at the end of its journey through the heart of the United States. Note the field patterns on either side of the river along its course, as farmers take advantage of the fertile soil deposited by past floods. Note the different shades of red in the fields, which indicate different crops at different stages of growth. Details within the city itself are harder to make out, with the exception of a white dot.

The Salton Sea, in southern California (center), was created in 1905/6 when a natural depression in this desert region was flooded from the south by water from the Colorado River. It is maintained at its present size, some 30 miles long and 10 miles wide (50 km by 16 km), by drainage from irrigated farmlands. The irrigated field patterns are clearly visible in this Landsat MSS image. In the north-west is the Coachella Valley, and in the south-east the larger Imperial Valley. Interestingly the irrigated land and intensive agriculture end abruptly on the US/Mexican border, reflecting the different farming practices of the two nations.

The shuttle imaging radar too can reveal differences in agricultural practice. This garishly false-colored radar scan of north-eastern Florida reveals a wealth of detail. The three lakes (above center) are Ocean Pond, Palestine Lake and Swift Creek Pond. The river (bottom) running into the Gulf of Mexico, is the Suwannee River. In the color code used here orange shows drainage channels. Dark green and purple are agricultural fields. Yellowish-green areas are stands of cypress drenched in early morning dew – the image was acquired at 3:59 am local time. Darkness is no barrier to radar scanning.

In the center-pivot irrigation system, water is pumped from below ground and broadcast over a circular area half a mile (0.8 km) across by a mobile sprinkler. As the photo shows, such a technique can make the desert bloom.

Shuttle astronauts on the 41-C mission photographed this extraordinary scene in the Saudi Arabian desert near Al Hufuf. The circular patches are in fact areas of land irrigated by the center-pivot irrigation method, originally designed for use in the American West.

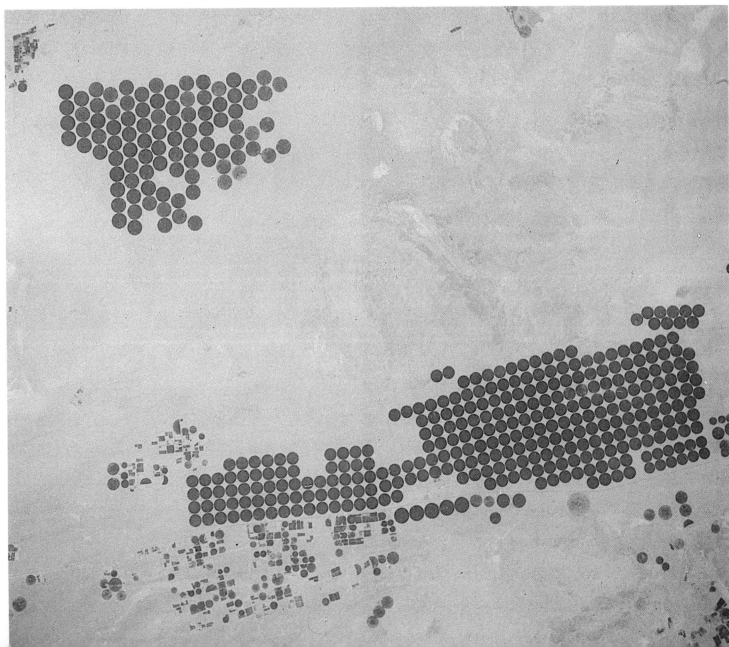

The Waters

Landsat images, though primarily concerned with land features, can also reveal plenty about the world's water resources. Hydrology – the study of inland waters – has been revolutionized by satellite data. Scientists can now see at a glance the water resources of a given area. In normal false-color imagery, water shows up black, but it can be highlighted in another color if required.

The water resources, of course, involve not only existing surface water, but 'potential' water trapped in snow and ice. The extent of snow cover and the rate of snow melt can be readily estimated from successive Landsat images. The onset of flooding, from rapid snow-melt or torrential rain, can also be quickly spotted, and steps taken to limit loss of life and damage to property. The overall picture seen from space can help pinpoint where to concentrate flood defenses.

Landsat's sensors can also peer into the water to see sediments. On suitably processed images, the sedimentation in estuaries and along the coasts can be easily traced. This is of particular interest to harbor engineers who have to keep navigation channels open.

Deadly Pollutants

In a similar way sources of pollution can be monitored. Raw sewage, industrial effluents, and oil slicks are readily detected by Landsat's multispectral eyes. Even the minute organic marine life, we know as plankton, does not evade discovery. Landsat images clearly show the periodic plankton 'blooms' that occur at sea, which naturally attract the attention of fish. This is just one of the ways remote sensing is helping the fisherman (see below).

Ship's navigators also have cause to thank Landsat, especially those sailing in the treacherous waters off north-east North America. The ever-present danger there is icebergs. Landsat provides early warning of their approach, and it actually spots where and when they calve from the glaciers. Landsat has also proved invaluable in bathymetry – the measurement of the ocean depths. In clear waters it can 'see' down to a depth of 10 fathoms (18 meters).

Seasat

To gain more detailed information about the oceans, which after all cover 70 per cent of the Earth's surface, NASA launched Seasat in 1978. Alas, it malfunctioned after only three months, but its results were spectacular.

Seasat was built up from an Agena rocket, and its most obvious feature was a large radar antenna. It used this radar to image coastal and land features and to determine the wavelength and direction of ocean waves. It carried radiometers that could measure the temperature of the sea to an accuracy of 2°C, and also measure the surface wind speeds very accurately.

The most remarkable results, however, came from a radar altimeter, which used radar pulses to measure Seasat's height above the waves. When the results were analysed, it was found that the sea surface actually dips in some parts of the ocean and rises in others! In places the sea surface height was as much as 16 ft (5 meters) higher or lower

Occupying the left half of this Landsat MSS image is the vast flood plane of the Yazoo Basin in the State of Mississippi. At the extreme left is the meandering Mississippi River itself, which forms the state boundary with Arkansas and Louisiana. For the time of the year when the image was obtained, June 1978, the basin is remarkably bare of vegetation. This is because the land is still recovering from widespread spring flooding. Without crop cover, innumerable oxbow lakes and ancient meanders of the river system in the basin show up.

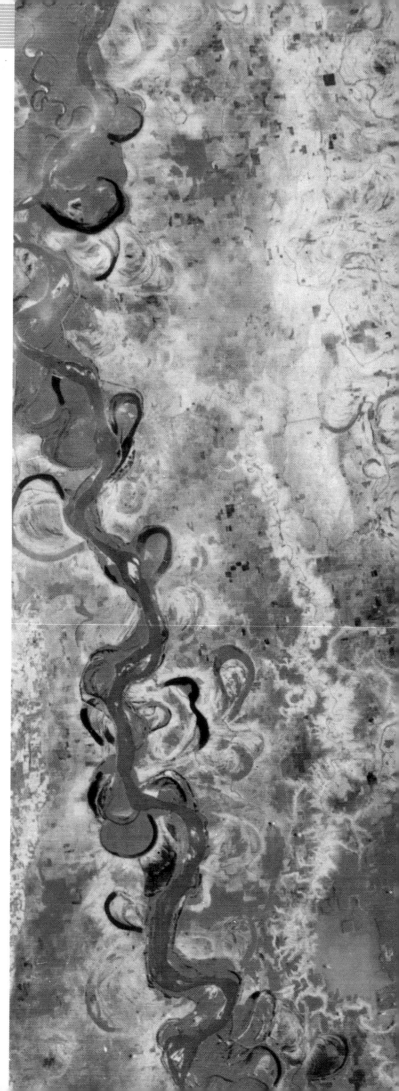

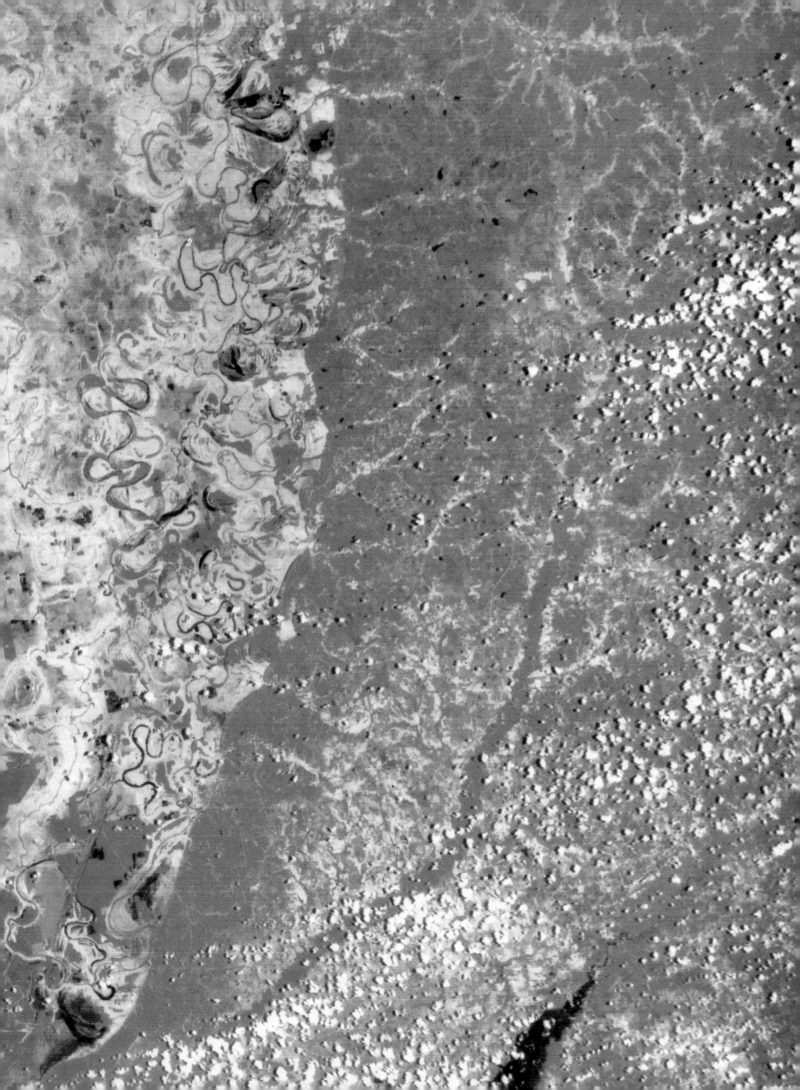

than mean sea level. What is happening is that the ocean surface rises and falls according to the rise and fall of the seabed beneath. So, in mapping the sea surface, Landsat also mapped the seabed – no mean feat from a height above sea level of 500 miles (800 km). See page 72.

Fishing from Space

The latest NOAA weather satellites also carry instruments that measure sea temperature. The temperature profile of the sea is of interest not only to weathermen, but also to fishermen. Fishermen use NOAA data to map the various eddies and currents of warm and cool waters that wander around the oceans. Knowing what temperatures fish prefer, they can follow these currents and stand more chance of good catches.

New York City and the Hudson River, viewed by Landsat's thematic mapper. Although short by North American standards (315 miles, 500 km), the Hudson proved a key factor in the opening up and development of the American Midwest and, of course, of New York City. The image has been color-coded to give a simulated natural color in which vegetation, for example, does appear green. Thus Central Park on Manhattan Island can easily be spotted, as can Prospect Park in Brooklyn. One of the most prominent features in the picture is Kennedy Airport (center right), whose runways are clearly visible.

For comparison, this is a NHAP photograph of Manhattan Island. It shows the extra detail you might expect from an airborne camera. Whereas Landsat takes its pictures from 435 miles (700 km) NHAP photographs are taken from only 7½ miles (12 km). Nevertheless the detail is perhaps greater than you would expect. You can clearly distinguish the twin towers of Manhattan's tallest skyscraper, the 1362-ft (415-m) World Trade Center, at the tip of the island.

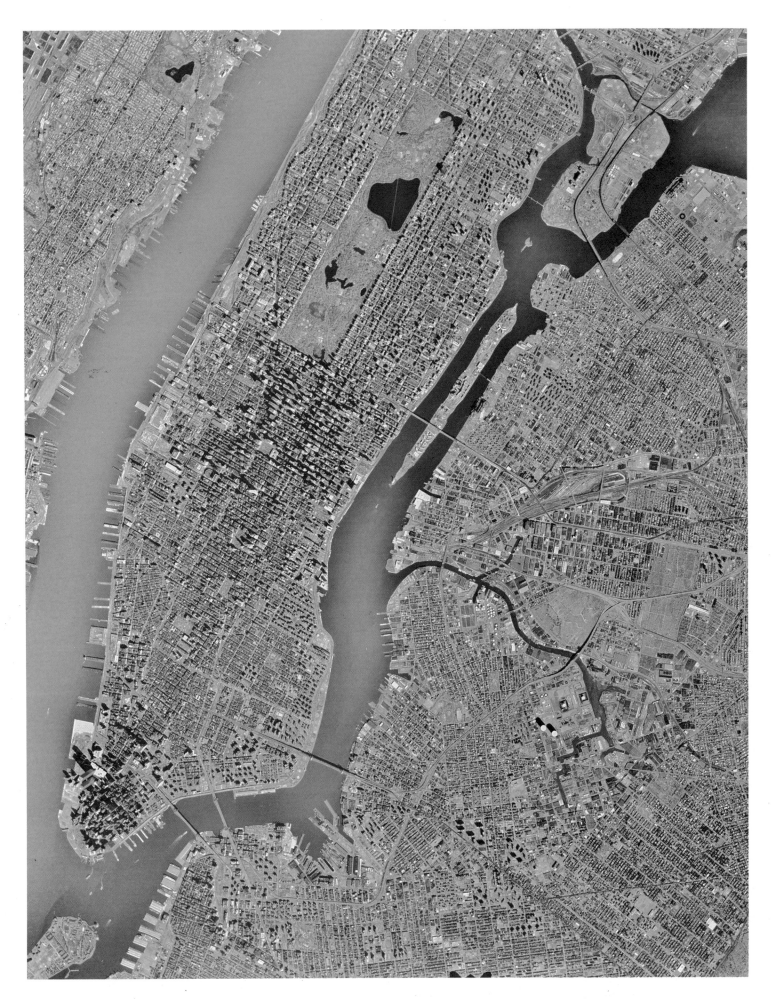

On the left of this Landsat MSS image is the vast delta region of the second largest river in China, the Hwang Ho. The name means 'Yellow River', and it is so called because of the considerable amount of yellowish silt it carries along its 3010 mile (4845 km) course to the Yellow Sea. You can see the silt (pale blue here) issuing from the numerous delta channels. Many, because of their straight course, are obviously man-made. To the south of this image is the North China Plain, known as China's granary because it is a major rice-growing area, benefiting from the fertile silt deposited by the Hwang Ho's regular flooding.

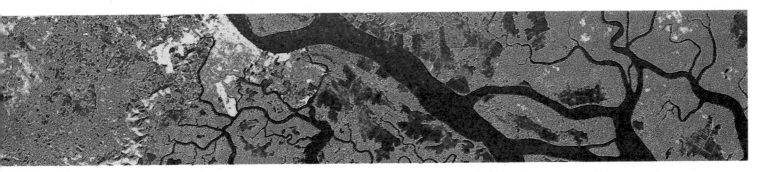

This shuttle imaging radar image around Ecuador's chief port Guayaquil (marked yellow, top center) shows rice cultivation as green patches on either side of the river (the Guayas), which flows from left to right. The purple and orange areas in the flood plain of the river show grazing land for beef cattle. The green areas on the left are forest land.

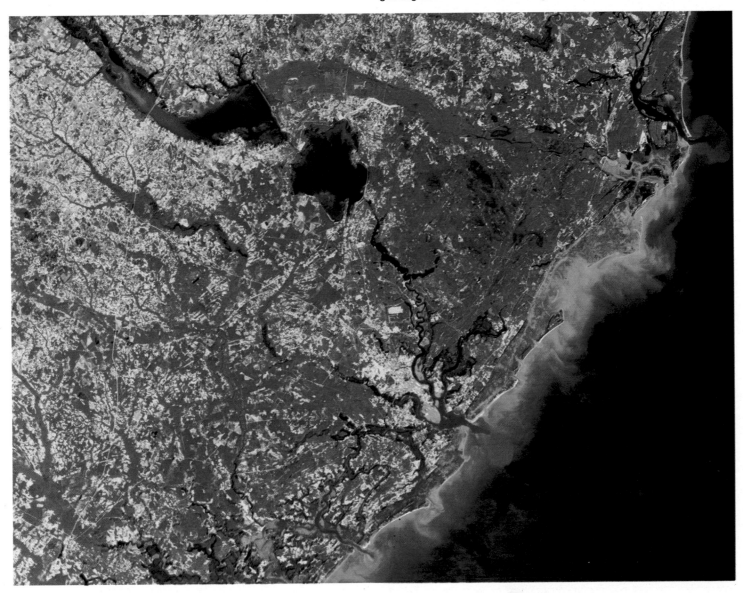

Most of the coast of South Carolina is seen in this Landsat thematic mapper image of the State's fertile Coastal Plains. Charleston is located two-thirds of the way down, at the mouth of the Cooper River. The most interesting feature of the coastline is the presence of sand bars. Behind them lagoons and tidal mud flats have formed from silt carried down by the rivers of the Plains. In time these flats will become permanent land as the sand bars form a new shoreline. There is evidence of parallel structure inland which were ancient shorelines.

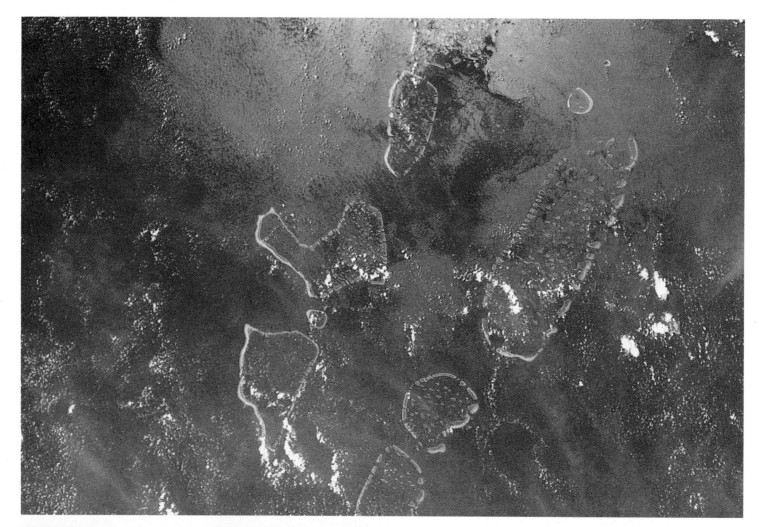

The Pacific Ocean is dotted with coral atolls. They are ring-shaped structures formed from the accumulated limy secretions of tiny creatures called polyps. Shuttle astronauts photographed this atoll group in the Maldive Island chain. As the atolls grow, they will start to trap flotsam and nuts and evolve into islands.

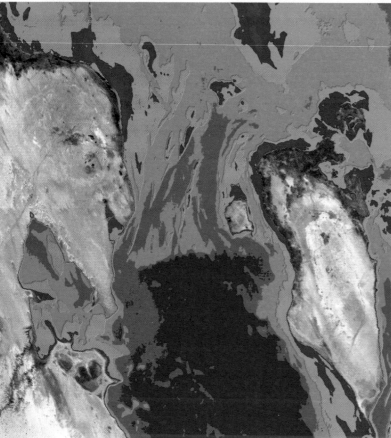

This is a Landsat image of the Persian Gulf, showing the island of Bahrain. It has been processed by the technique of density slicing to show water depths around the island. Under favorable conditions Landsat can 'see' down to a depth of 10 fathoms (20 meters) or more. (For comparison a normal Landsat image of the region can be seen on page 29).

Key (depths in fathoms)
Red = 0-1   Brown = 1-3
Pale blue = 3-5   Medium blue = 5-10
Dark blue = >10

No coral polyps made this group of islands! The British Isles form part ▶ of the continental shelf of Europe and were once linked to the mainland. The main island of Great Britain (England, Wales and Scotland) is Europe's largest island and the eighth largest in the world. This image is a mosaic produced from the 52 Landsat images that cover the area. It is printed in simulated natural color. Geographers and geologists frequently use mosaics to get a better overall picture of ground features.

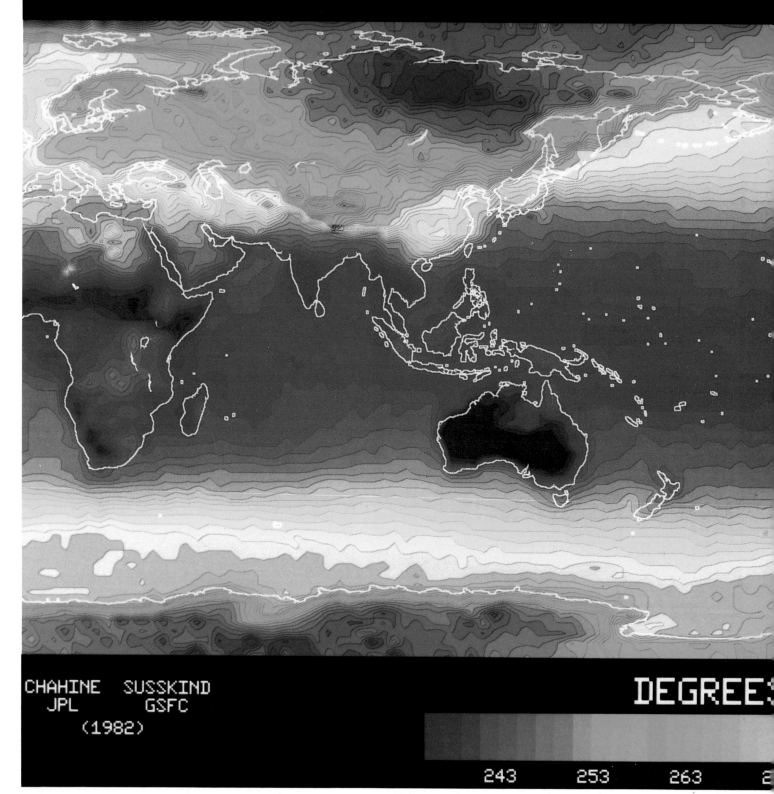

MEAN SURFACE TEMPERA
FROM HIRS

CHAHINE   SUSSKIND
   JPL   GSFC
      (1982)

DEGREE

243   253   263

The data used to prepare this global picture of surface temperatures were obtained from instruments carried by a Tiros N/NOAA weather satellite, the HIRS (high-resolution infrared sounder) and the MSU (microwave sounding unit). The satellite orbited at a height of some 540 miles (870 km). The picture again graphically illustrates the advantages of color-coding techniques to present data.

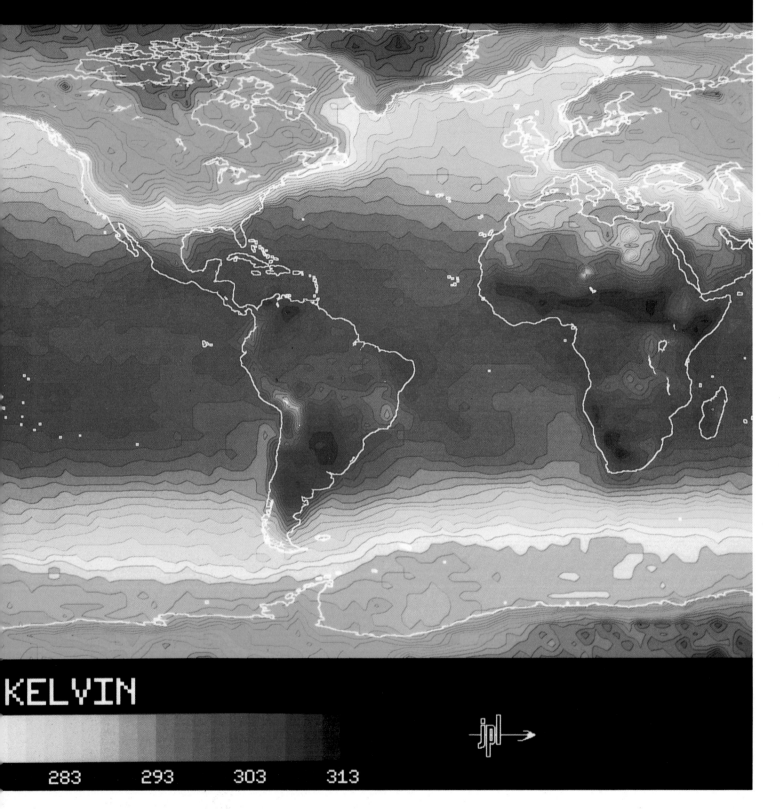

KELVIN

283   293   303   313

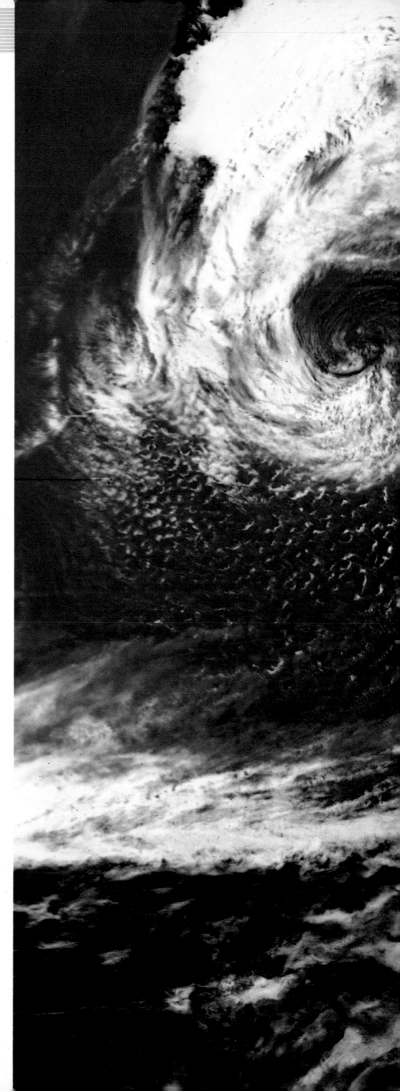

The Weather Eye

Clouds, as far as Landsat is concerned, are a nuisance. Its sensors are unable to see through these gigantic puffballs of water droplets and ice crystals. But to the weatherman, clouds, and the way they move, hold the key to the understanding of the weather system. Weathermen, or meteorologists as they are properly called, do not use Landsat to take cloud pictures over the Earth, but purpose-build weather satellites.

NASA launched an experimental weather satellite, Tiros 1, in 1960. This provided meteorologists with the first ever near-global picture of world weather systems, as revealed by cloud formations riding on invisible winds. Weather study was revolutionized overnight. For the first time meteorologists could spot where weather systems were being born – in the middle of remote oceans where there were no weather stations. And they could trace the development of these systems day by day.

Tiros

A string of Tiros satellites followed, (Tiros stands for television and infrared observation satellite). The latest type in the series is the Tiros N, which is a far cry from the first one. Tiros N satellites are designated NOAA in orbit, after the government agency that operates them, the National Oceanographic and Atmospheric Administration. NOAA satellites are highly sophisticated sensing robots that can do much more than just take cloud pictures in the daylight. They take cloud pictures by day and by night. They record the temperature of the surface and the temperature and moisture content at different levels in the atmosphere.

In addition, NOAA satellites carry equipment to relay information from fixed and moving weather platforms in remote areas. These record such things as local temperature, pressure, rainfall and snow depth. Some of the latest NOAA craft have additional communications equipment tuned to the frequency of the emergency radio locator beacons carried by ships and planes. They form part of a search and rescue satellite (sarsat) system, operated in conjunction with Russian craft, such as Cospas.

NOAA satellites sense the Earth as they orbit over the poles at a height of about 500 miles (800 km). They view virtually all the surface at least twice every 24 hours. They broadcast their instrument readings continuously, which are available free, to anyone with suitable antennas. These cloud-cover pictures in particular can be received on relatively inexpensive ground equipment through the so-called APT (Automatic Picture Transmission) system.

With their global coverage and data distribution, the NOAAs are currently the most important of all weather satellites. However, the United States and several other nations now also use other satellites that give a more local view of the weather situation. These satellites are located 22,300 miles (35,900 km) high in geostationary orbits over the equator, which means they appear 'fixed' in the sky. They look down on a whole hemisphere and provide pictures of it every half-hour.

GOES Satellites

The United States operates two such satellites, called GOES, one to the east and one to the west of the continent. Another satellite named Meteosat, keeps a permanent eye over the weather of Europe, Africa and the Middle East; while a Japanese satellite, GMS, monitors the Pacific region. As a result, apart from small areas near the poles, the whole global weather system is under permanent observation.

No winds spring up, no hurricanes form, no ocean currents change direction without being scrutinized from above.

Winding itself up as it spirals around an area of low pressure, a vast cyclonic weather system bears down on Western Europe from the North Atlantic. The heavy storm front is already affecting Ireland and most of Scotland. The first Tiros N weather satellite imaged this classic weather system with its advanced radiometer.

GOES weather satellites like this one, together with the Tiros N series, form the mainstay of American weather monitoring program. They operate from stationary orbit above the equator over the Atlantic and Pacific Oceans. Some 7 ft (2.2 meters) in diameter and 12 ft (3.6 meters) tall, they have an operational life of seven years.

Carrying a GOES weather satellite, a Delta launch vehicle blasts off from the launch site at Cape Canaveral. All GOES satellites take off from the Cape, which is the most suitable US launch site for satellites destined for stationary orbit. Delta is perhaps the most successful of all conventional launch vehicles with well over 150 successful launches to its credit.

From their 22,300-mile (35,900-km) high orbit over the equator, GOES satellites scan a complete hemisphere in just half an hour. They return data from their monitoring instruments which can produce images in three wavebands, including the visible. The visible image provides the cloud cover pictures weather forecasters use on television. This cloud picture, showing the weather systems over the Americas, was imaged by GOES 4, located over the Pacific Ocean.

Shuttle astronauts have a different perspective on the weather. Using ordinary color film, the 51-A crew captured this dramatic scene of towering cumulus clouds above Argentina, tinted by the setting Sun.

This image was also taken by GOES 4 in stationary orbit to the west of the Americas. It shows a nearly cloud-free United States from Mexico to the Canadian border. But there are dense storm centers in the Gulf of Mexico and the eastern Caribbean.

This view of the eastern United States and Caribbean region has also been obtained from the GOES 4 data. It shows the weather systems in more detail. The huge spiral of cloud over Hispaniola and Puerto Rico (center right) is actually a hurricane, Hurricane David. It was the most destructive of the 1979 season. In this image the central core measures 250 miles (400 km) across.

The European weather satellite Meteosat took this image of Europe, Africa and the Middle East at infrared wavelengths. Vivid false coloration makes the hot land masses stand out. A simulated natural color image produced from other data received at the same time is shown on pages 8-9.

A Tiros-N type weather satellite, which circles the Earth in polar orbit. They are operated by NOAA, the National Oceanographic and Atmospheric Administration, and in orbit are designated by NOAA numbers. They carry a range of highly sensitive monitoring instruments and have the added capability for collecting data from remote weather platforms. The latest versions also carry equipment to monitor emergency frequencies for ships and aircraft in distress. This is part of a joint search and rescue satellite (sarsat) program with the Russians.

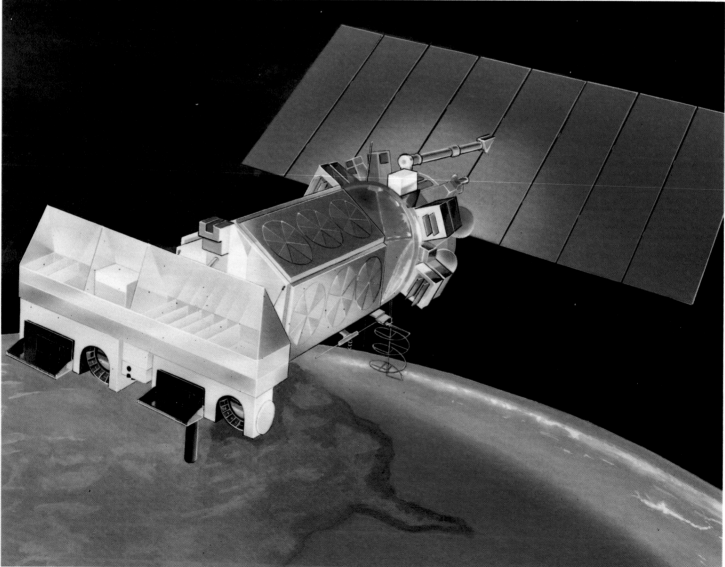

Among the instruments on board the NOAA series of weather satellites is an advanced very high resolution radiometer (AVHRR). This simulated natural color image was produced from data returned from NOAA 7's AVHRR. It shows the eastern Mediterranean under the cloudless skies to be expected there at the time the image was acquired, July. Visible on the east coast of the island of Sicily, at the tip of the 'boot' of Italy, is the circular structure of Mount Etna, a regularly active volcano. You can see a Skylab photograph of Etna on page 25.

Catastrophe

Throughout history 'acts of God' such as earthquakes, volcanoes, hurricanes, floods and drought have wreaked havoc on mankind. And they continue to do so. We have no more control over the forces that have shaped our planet since its creation than our caveman ancestors. All we can do is watch and wait and try to predict when such natural disasters may strike. We can do little about them when they do.

Remote sensing from orbit can play a part in disaster-warning schemes, especially as far as the weather is concerned. Weather satellites spot where hurricanes and typhoons are born over tropical oceans, and track them as they wind themselves up, ready to unleash their fury over the land. Communities in their path can then be warned and evacuated.

Disaster Warnings

Early warnings have saved tens of thousands of lives since the beginning of the space age. But tragically some go unheeded, as happened in Bangladesh in May 1985. Warnings were given of a powerful cyclone approaching from the sea. But most of the population in the low coastal areas ignored the warning, believing that this cyclone would miss them as other cyclones had before. This one didn't. On May 24 it stormed in with a 45 ft (14 meter) high tidal wave. Within a few hours perhaps as many as 40,000 people were dead and a quarter of a million people made homeless.

At present, remote sensing cannot help warn of earthquakes and volcanoes. But it does give geologists a much better picture of the structure of the rocks in the danger zones, which can also help them understand the phenomena better. Remote sensing is also invaluable in monitoring the impact of such events on the landscape.

Mount St Helens

This was vividly demonstrated after the multimegaton eruption of Mount St Helens, in Washington State, on May 18, 1980. On that day the picture-postcard conical summit of the mountain blasted itself apart, releasing billowing clouds of hot ash 12 miles (20 km) into the air. The dust rained down inches thick for hundreds of miles around, and buried 6000 miles (9500 km) of roads. Fifty-seven people were killed – buried by mud slides, burned by ash, or suffocated by fumes. The pictures over the page show the devastation caused. Ominously, almost five years to the day after the 1980 eruption, a bulge began to appear in the crater, showing that Mount St Helens is still very much alive.

Nemesis!

Landsat images also tell of natural cataclysmic events that originated out of this world. They show where, millions of years ago, gigantic meteorites, comets or asteroids, have impacted the Earth. The most famous of all craters gouged out by cosmic impact is the Meteorite Crater in Arizona.

Although over 4000 ft (1200 meters) across, it is dwarfed by other ancient craters that have long since filled in and become part of the landscape. One of the most impressive of these is the Manicouagon crater, located in Canada just north of the mouth of the St Lawrence

On May 18, 1980 an explosion with 500 times the power of the Hiroshima atomic bomb blasted the top 1300 ft (400 meters) from Mount St Helens in Washington State. This long dormant volcano was the first to erupt in the continental United States since Mount Lassen was active in 1914. Both are in the Cascade Range, which extends for more than 700 miles (1100 km) from northern California into British Columbia. NASA was actively involved in monitoring the eruption and its aftermath from aircraft, spacecraft and balloons.

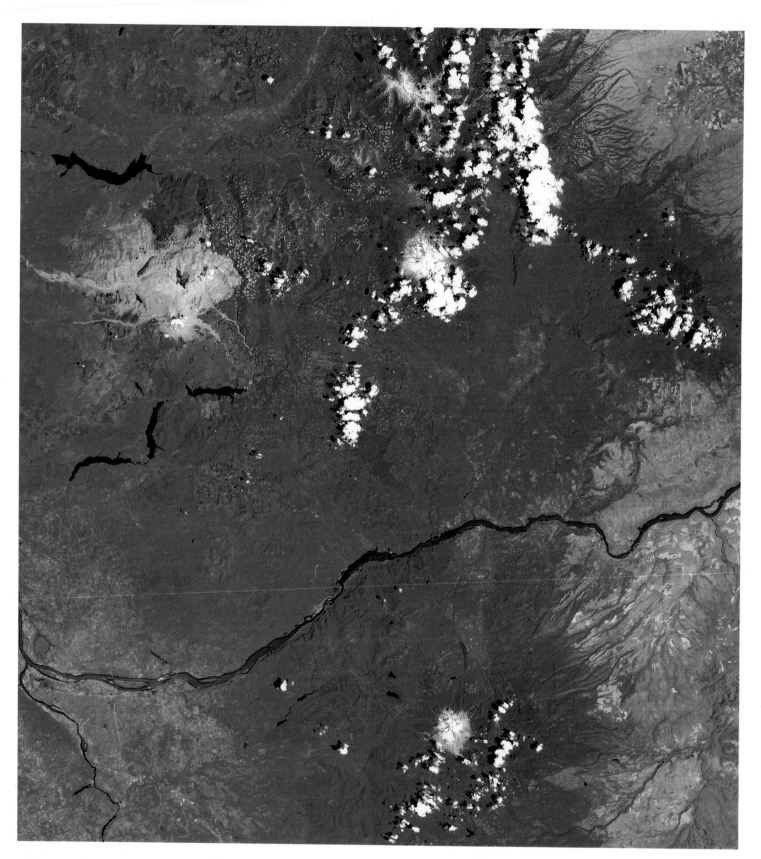

This Landsat view imaged 14 months after the event, shows
the havoc wreaked by the Mount St Helens eruption of May 1980. The
countryside around the mountain is thickly covered with ash. And ash
chokes the streams leaving the slopes. What was once Spirit Lake
immediately north of the crater is now a vast mud pool. During the
eruption the ash was blown north-east, and fell like dirty snow on
townships in its path. One of the worst places hit was Yakima (top
right), where at noon on May 18 day turned into night.

River. It measures 40 miles (64 km) across. Imagine the destruction and loss of life that would follow such an impact on a metropolis today.

Recent theories suggest that we may soon, geologically speaking, be due for another onslaught from space, perhaps in about 13 million years. It would be triggered off by an as yet undiscovered companion star of the Sun called Nemesis. This would disturb the cloud of comets believed to exist in the outer reaches of the solar system, and hurl them towards the Sun. The Earth and the other planets would experience deadly bombardment, which would cause on Earth the extinction of many species, perhaps even of the human race.

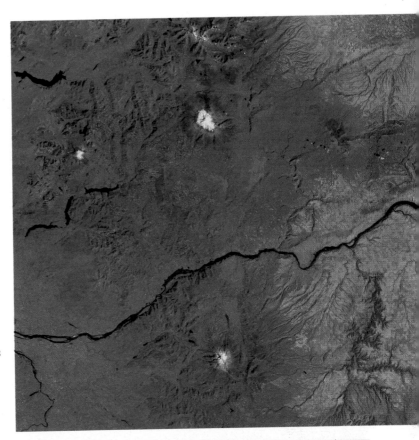

In September 1979 this is what the Mount St Helens region of the Cascade Range looked like. The mountain is located at top left; Mount Adams is on the right, and Mount Hood is near the bottom. Cutting through the image is the Columbia River, marking the Oregon State line. The city of Portland is to the bottom left.

This is a NASA aerial view of Mount St Helens only a month after the eruption, taken from 60,000 ft (18,000 meters). A pall of steam still hangs over the crater. Within the areas covered by ash there is no sign of vegetation, which would appear red in this infrared image. It is interesting now to look at the Landsat image taken over a year later. You can see patches of red appearing in the gray on the lower slopes, showing that nature is re-establishing itself slowly but surely.

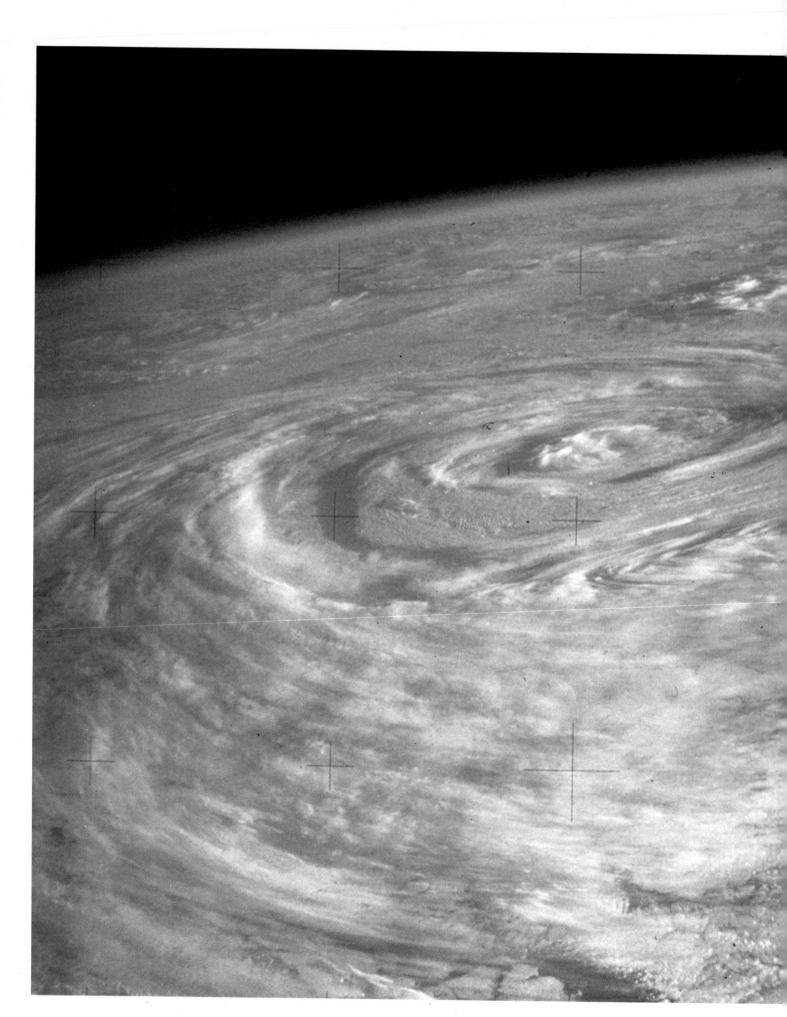

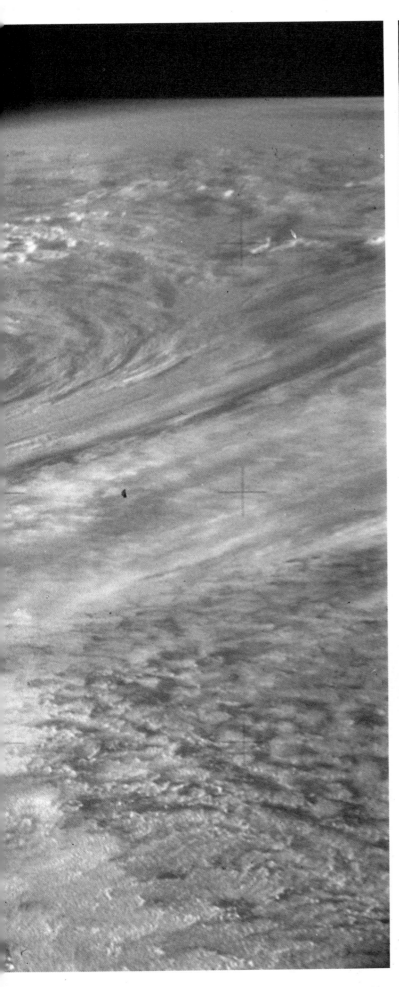

The shuttle astronaut's view of destructive weather systems is also fascinating. On Mission 51-A the astronauts spied this cyclone over the Marianas Islands in the East Pacific Ocean. Terrestrial meteorologists knew it as Typhoon Bill. Note the very prominent 'eye' around which the winds spiral.

Having taken the full force of a hurricane's fury, these wooden homes on the coast of the Gulf of Mexico in Texas, lie in total ruin.

Skylab astronauts photographed this gigantic tropical storm system over the South Pacific Ocean in 1973. Due to the low Sun angle, this natural color photograph looks almost three-dimensional. The relief is provided by towering cumulonimbus thunderclouds penetrating a layer of high cirrus clouds.

This Landsat MSS image shows some of the interesting canyon lands in central Arizona between Flagstaff (near top left) and Phoenix (just out of the picture left). But the most noteworthy feature by far is the huge circular crater just below top center. It is the famous Arizona Meteorite Crater, the result of bombardment by a gigantic lump of rock from outer space, probably more than 25,000 years ago. Should a large meteorite hit a built-up area today it would cause immense devastation and kill perhaps millions of people.

An aerial view of the Arizona Meteorite crater, which shows how well preserved it is, considering its age. The crater measures some 4150 ft (1205 meters) across and is 575 ft (175 meters) deep. NASA has a connection here too because the Apollo astronauts trained in the crater in preparation for their Moon-walking excursions, since it resembles a typical lunar crater.

One of the ever-present catastrophies in Africa is drought, with both Sudan and Ethiopia suffering badly recently as the seasonal rains have failed year after year. This lack of precious water can be monitored from space in the gradual reduction of the sizes of lakes and reservoirs. The shuttle 41-C astronauts took this photograph of Lake Chad in 1984. Estimates put its area at only about 1000 square miles (2600 square kilometers). Yet when Gemini 7 astronauts photographed the Lake in 1965, it had at least seven times the area.

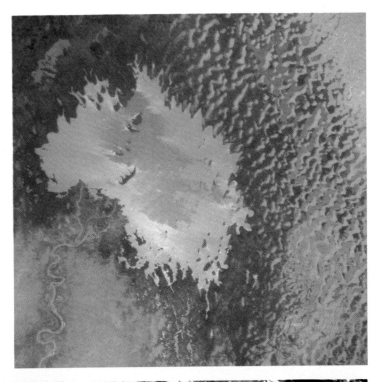

Among the man-made catastrophes to befall us, oil pollution at sea is becoming increasingly common, to the detriment of beach and coastal life. Estimating the extent of an oil spill from a tanker or an offshore well is another task that can be carried out from orbit by suitably processing spacecraft data. This picture shows in red the oil slick from Iran's Nowruz offshore oilfield in the Persian Gulf in spring 1983. Three wells there were damaged earlier in the year, one by a storm and two by Iraqi gunships. The image was obtained by processing AVHRR data from NOAA 7.

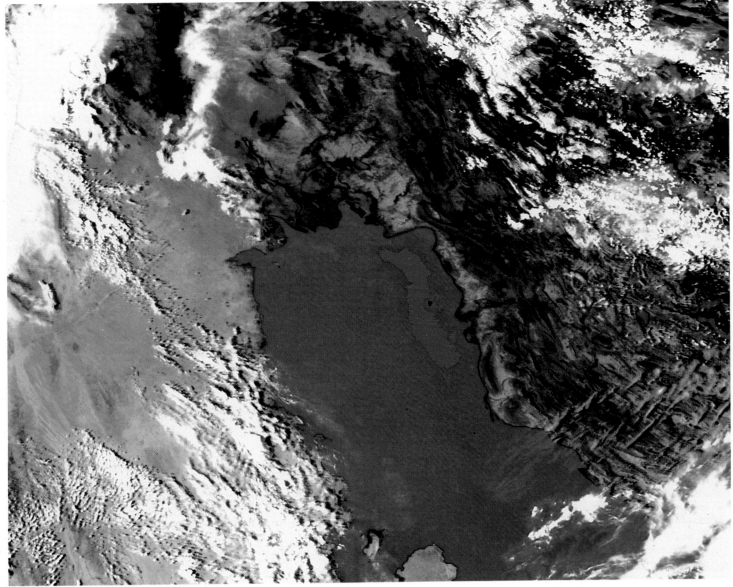

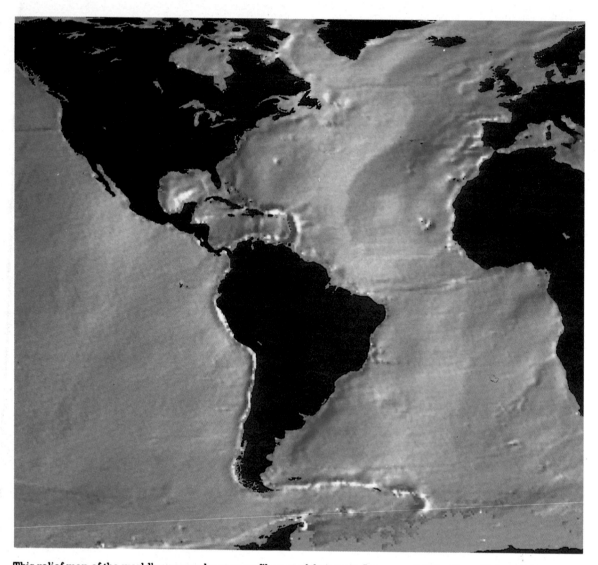

This relief map of the world's oceans shows a profile, not of the ocean floor, as might be thought, but of the ocean surface! Unbelievably, it shows that the ocean surface actually dips in regions where there are deep trenches in the seabed. It was prepared from data returned by a remarkable satellite called Seasat.

Endpapers: Part of the Hammersley mountain range in Western Australia, as viewed by the shuttle imaging radar. The image has been color coded to show differences in topography.

PICTURE CREDITS

The author and publishers would like to thank the EROS Data Center, Sioux Falls, South Dakota, and the Remote Sensing Unit, RAE Farnborough, England, for processing the Landsat images included in the book. They would also like to thank NASA for providing the Skylab, shuttle and shuttle imaging radar pictures. Aerial photography is by NASA and US Geological Survey. Thanks are also due to the following for supplying other photographs: **Aldus Archive/BPCC** 27 top, U.S.G.S 27 center left **Daily Telegraph Colour Library** 29 top **European Space Agency** 8, 9, 62 top **EROS Data Center** 11, 12 13 bottom **Hughes Aerospace** 10, 58 top right, 59 top **The Image Bank** Alvis Upitis 69 bottom **Robin Kerrod** 30 bottom, 70 bottom **Science Photo Library** 45 top, 64-65

Multimedia Publications have endeavored to observe the legal requirements with regard to the suppliers of photographic material.